PRAISE FOR BARRY FRIEDMAN AND HIS BOOKS

"No one I know of has honored a father as gallantly as has Barry Friedman, animating 'the oddities and wonders of Jack Friedman' for readers whose misfortune was never to have met him. Jack's enormous success was to have raised a son who loved him so faithfully, so drolly, and—our reward—so memorably."

— MARK SINGER, AUTHOR OF *FUNNY MONEY* AND STAFF WRITER FOR *THE NEW YORKER*

"You can't go on the road with standup comedian Barry Friedman, which is probably good for your health and sanity. But you can feel what it felt like, through this funny, gritty, wondrously detailed and scarily honest book I really am enjoying it."

— DAVE BARRY, AUTHOR, RECIPIENT OF THE PULITZER PRIZE AND THE WALTER CRONKITE AWARD FOR EXCELLENCE IN JOURNALISM (ABOUT *THE JOKE WAS ON ME*)

"From the Baby O! Lounge in Hastings, Nebraska to the Elks Lodge in Seminole, Oklahoma, it's Barry Friedman! Let's give him a big hand, folks. He's written a book with all the wisdom and humanity of Alexis de Tocqueville's Democracy in America, but with way better jokes and twice as many clitoral piercings."

— JOHN H. RICHARDSON (ABOUT *THE JOKE WAS ON ME*)

"This masterpieces would blow away the competition, if there were competition for such a masterpiece, which there is not."

— SHANE GERICKE, BESTSELLING AUTHOR OF *THE FURY* (ABOUT *JACOB FISHMAN'S MARRAIGES*)

"Seeing the broken yet still beautiful work through Barry's eyes is cathartic"

— JENNIFER TAUB, AUTHOR OF *BIG DIRTY MONEY* (ABOUT *JACOB FISHMAN'S MARRIAGES*)

"I knew this book would be special after reading the first sentence — 'You died today.' I was right. In *Four Days and a Year Later*, every single word counts. Barry Friedman invites readers to bear witness as he opens his heart and soul and pulls no punches in telling a story of loss and survival that is both tragic and inspirational. This book is simply incredible. What a gift Friedman has created for us."

— MICHAEL WALLIS, AUTHOR, *THE BEST LAND UNDER HEAVEN: THE DONNER PARTY IN THE AGE OF MANIFEST DESTINY*

"I haven't been able to get five pages in without having to catch my breath. You're a brave writer, my brother."

— CHARLES P. PIERCE, *ESQUIRE* (ABOUT *FOUR DAYS AND A YEAR LATER*)

"[*Four Days and a Year Later*] is a shattering memoir about love and parenthood and all the ways you can love too much and still lose everything. For anyone struggling to understand the current drug crisis and anyone trying to imagine the outer edges of family this book will both sear and hold you. Powerful, brutally self aware, Barry Friedman is a flashlight through loss and redemption"

— DAHLIA LITHWICK, SENIOR EDITOR, *SLATE*

JACK SH*T

Connie + John -
Across the hall
  neighbors

Thank you.

JACK SH*T

VOLUPTUOUS BAGELS AND OTHER CONCERNS
OF JACK FRIEDMAN

VOLUME ONE

BARRY FRIEDMAN

BABYLON
BOOKS

To Florence Friedman, Jack Friedman's wife, my mother. Dad was right, Ma, when he used to scream at God. "What, He couldn't give her 10 more years? It would have killed him." You would have enjoyed your husband the 23 years you've been gone. And it wouldn't have killed Him.

1

2004-2012

F ive years after my mother died from breast-to-bone cancer, my father decided to sell the townhome they owned in Mays Landing, New Jersey, about 45 minutes from Atlantic City, and move to Las Vegas.

He was 78.

And when I say he decided to move, I decided he should move. As a standup comedian, I was working in Vegas in the mid-2000s approximately 30 weeks a year, and I knew he liked it there. He used to meet me at the MGM or the Riviera or the Maxim, wherever my gig was — before and after my mother died — and come to shows. His game, which he also played in Atlantic City, was $5 Craps, which he called "Crap," not as a commentary as much as never quite being sure whether the game was plural or not. Southern Jersey was too cold and filled with too many memories and, in his case, stairs. The townhome was three levels, and while hearing him moan, sometimes in person, sometimes on the phone, about having to schlep up and down those "goddamn stairs" was hilarious, I did worry about this elderly man with an ill-fitting toupee (and much more of that to come) someday actually doing a nosedive down one of those stairs, his "Oy" going unheeded for days. Even before my mother, his wife, died (and as this book goes on and my father's memory started to fade, it was important to remind him that that woman was one and the same), he enjoyed Las Vegas and said he wouldn't mind living there someday. He enjoyed having a son who was a standup comedian in town, but he loved having a son who was a standup comedian in Vegas who got him buffet comps.

"Nobody's paying for these, Ba?" he'd say as we walked into the buffets at the various hotels at which I was working and handed the vouchers to the cashier.

"They give 'em to comedians, Dad."

"You got enough? I'd hate to take them from you."

"You're not. It's fine."

"Why?"

" 'Why?' "

"Yeah, why?"

"Why do I have them? Because they give them to me."

"For free?"

"For free."

"Wow-e-wow!"

"Dad, the food, let's face it, is usually pretty awful."

"Yeah, but you got the variety."

∾

THE TOWNHOME in Jersey sold within weeks of listing it. I then agreed to meet him in Vegas to help him find a place to live.

∾

"BA, we've got to move fast," he said in the hotel the night before we were to start looking.

"Dad, your house doesn't close for 90 days. We don't have to move fast."

"I know, but I'm saying. We have to move fast."

"We really don't. We're not laundering money here."

"I don't mean fast fast, but, you know, we have to move fast."

"Say it again, please."

"I'm just saying we have to find something."

"We'll find something. We don't have to take the first thing we see."

～

WE TOOK the third thing we saw.

His first residence in Las Vegas was a two-bedroom apartment in Summerlin, west of the Strip and just east of Interstate 215, on South Pavilion Center Drive. The address was important because it was across the street, albeit a very busy and wide street, from the Red Rock Casino.

～

"YOU KNOW, Ba, I could walk there."

"No, you couldn't."

"Yes, it's right there."

"Dad, it's about a half a mile, door to door, from your apartment to the casino. You cannot walk there."

"You don't know what you're talking about."

"Have you ever walked there?"

"That's not the point!"

"That is actually exactly the point. Have you ever walked there?"

"I nearly did once."

"When?"

"I don't know, I did."

"My point, Dad, is you can't walk there."

"You don't know what you're talking about. I could walk there."

THESE WERE good years for him, the early ones in Vegas, at this apartment and at the house he would eventually buy. He would head almost daily not to the Red Rock, which he reminded me repeatedly was within walking distance from his apartment, but to the Suncoast Casino, about a 15-minute drive away. There, he told me, they treated him like a big shot.

"They give me anything I want," he used to tell me. "I haven't paid for a meal in, like, 10 years."

"You've only been here for three."

"You know what I mean."

I'D COME out to see him, even when I wasn't performing, as would my brother, Wayne (whom my father would occasionally call Bernie, my father's dead cousin), who lived in California, and my sister, Susan (whom he would occasionally call Cynthia, my father's dead niece), who lived on Long Island.

He also joined a tennis league.

"You're playing tennis, Dad?"

"Yeah, I got a group. They're retired, you know, the oldsters. We play four-game sets."

"Four-game sets? What is that?"

"You know, the four games."

"But what if there's a tie?"

"What kind of tie?"

"A tie — two-games-apiece kind of thing."

"We play, we don't play."

"OK."

"Oh, listen, one guy, Ba, is a retired Air Force pilot. Can you believe it?"

"Why wouldn't I believe it?"

"Wait, wait. He's Jewish. Who ever heard of a Jewish Air Force pilot? I do his taxes. I don't charge him."

My father, at the time, was a semiretired accountant, which was frightening and got more frightening as the years went on.

"Good that you got a group of guys to play tennis with."

"You can't play during the day here in Vegas. It's murderous with this heat. That's why we play four-game sets. Doubles."

"Again with the four-game sets."

"No, it's fun. I don't run after the ball, though."

"Why not?"

"When they pay, I'll run after it."

"That's the spirit."

"Anyway, nothing special. But how about that? A pilot?"

"Amazing."

"A Jewish pilot. I can't get over that. I'll be a son of a gun."

FOR A MAN in his late seventies, my father was in remarkable shape. He'd still make occasional trips back to New York for the few clients he had left, one of whom was a Serbian doctor named Petar who spoke broken English. My father was hard of hearing. Their conversations were stellar. This one was on speaker.

"Jack, hi!"

"Who's this?"

"Petar!"

"Petar?"

"Petar! Jack, it's Petar!"

"Oh, Peter. How goes your life?"

"What?"

"I say, 'What's new?' "

"I got a letter from the IRS. They say I don't—"

"The who?"

"The New York State Department of—"

"Who?"

"The New York—"

"You talked to who?"

"The New York State—"

"—Put it in an envelope and send—"

"What?"

"Send it to me."

"Send it to you?"

"What?"

"Send you the . . . the . . . —"

"Yeah, I don't know what it is, though, until I look at it. But don't worry about it. They probably want something."

When he got the phone call and when he got off the phone, he relayed to me the whole conversation — the one I just heard because my father had Petar on speaker. For 35 years, my father had Petar for a client, and for 35 years my father spelled his name "Peter" on tax returns.

"You know, Dad," I'd say on those occasions when I'd help him put the information on the computer on which he reluctantly started doing tax work, "it's Petar with an 'a,' not an 'e.' "

"That doesn't matter."

"Maybe to Petar it does."

"The government doesn't care."

"You sure?"

"You think they're going to care?"

"Yeah."

"So what are you doing on the computer? You know, I don't use them."

"Dad, I know, but it's easier this way because the tax program figures out all the calculations."

"Yeah, I know, but I don't use them."

"I know, but this is why you should."

"So what do you do? You put in the numbers and then you electrify it?"

"Yeah, I'm going to electrify it and then send it in."

"How do you do that?"

"You hit the 'send' button."

"Who would have thought of that?"

"Remember, technology is not your friend."

"What does it want from my life?"

"Don't worry. But we should really start spelling people's name's right. Don't forget that woman who came over."

"What woman?"

"The woman last week whose taxes you were doing."

"Oh, her. She was confused."

"Dad, you had her birthday wrong, you said she was a widow, and you forgot to include some of her income."

"She was confused, but I explained it to her. You don't have to get these forms right."

"You what? Of course you do."

"If we don't and they don't like it, the IRS will send him a letter."

You can't get tax advice like that anymore.

He was at the apartment on South Pavilion Center Drive for about four years, but with interest rates low and the Las Vegas and Summerlin housing market stagnant, I suggested to him that he buy a house.

"What do I want with a house?"

"You don't want a house?"

"I mean, it's not that I don't want a house, but . . . a house?"

"Yeah, a house."

"A house?"

"A house."

This was how our conversations went through the years.

"Maybe you should invest in something instead of throwing your money away on rent."

"You know I'm throwing my money away on rent, maybe I should buy something. You know, I've been thinking about that."

"Of course you have."

I had dear friends in Las Vegas, Bruce and Vicki, both real estate agents and both of whom said they'd help my father buy a place, a job that fell mostly to Vicki. I told her this might be the quickest deal she ever made.

He bought the second house he saw.

Vicki, this Vicki, was only his third-favorite Vicki. His favorite, Vicki Schwartz, was a woman he was dating at the time; coming in at No. 2 was Vicki Mustard — no lie, that was her name — a woman he had met somewhere. And my Vicki was his third.

"I'm going to become his favorite Vicki," she said, "if it kills me."

THE HOUSE on Tumble Brook Drive was a two-bedroom, 1,100 square feet. He used to tell people he lived in a big house.

"Yeah, yeah, I got two bathrooms, a living room, two bedrooms."

And it was only five minutes away from the Suncoast. After he moved in, he joined another Survivors Group, more men and women who had lost their husbands and wives over the years. The group included Carol, whom my father told me was married to a man collecting disability and an Army pension after a jeep fell on him ("But she won't sleep with him," he told me); Bill, a retired cop from Indiana, and his wife, Cindy, whom my father said "wasn't all there"; Ivan, another retired military man, who liked to shoot guns; Doug, a cheap bigot, who was dating Velma, who eventually dumped Doug and then married a priest who left the church; and Jeannette, the woman my father started dating who lived in a trailer in a mobile-home park and who (this was always added) "buried two husbands."

"You know, Ba, she's not Jewish," he told me once about Jeannette. "She's got a cross."

"Most Jews don't," I said.

"So I told her under no circumstances was I converting."

"Did she ask you to?"

"But I told her anyway. A cross she wears, nu?"

"Leave her alone."

"I need a cross. Don't misunderstand me. I'm not knocking it."

"It sounds like you're knocking it."

"Ah, c'mon."

"You enjoy her company?"

"There's no sex."

"I need that image."

"What?"

"You know what."

"Listen, I know you think you're the only one, but remember something — in my day, there was plenty of tumulting."

"Tumulting?"

"Yeah, you know, sex — bullshit, bullshit."

"I know, but I don't think that's the word you're looking for."

"But she's nice, she's very accommodating. But she buys food in the Dollar Store. I tell her, 'There's no meat on this chicken.' "

"You told her that?"

"The chicken. You can barely eat it. I tell her to stop buying food there."

"Do you thank her at least for making you dinner?"

"I thank her, but it's not very good."

"You're missing the point here."

"Listen, if she asks you to dinner, politely beg off. Tell her you have something with the show. Frankly, I can't stand eating there."

One Easter, Jeannette in fact invited us for dinner, but my father had special buffet coupons from the Suncoast, so he called her to tell her we weren't coming.

"Listen, about dinner, I don't think we can make it tonight. I have some tax clients coming in and they want to go over some things — you know, tax work."

He got off the phone.

"You don't think she really believed you, do you?"

"What am I going to do? Did I tell you about the chicken?"

"Yes, you told me about the chicken, but maybe she wasn't going to make chicken tonight."

"No, it's all right. I'll see her this week. And she's going to make chicken."

"How do you know she's going to make chicken?"

"She makes it. She gets it at the Dollar Store."

The buffets, though, to him: life itself. He didn't go just to eat; he went to win. I got a call one day in Tulsa.

"Ba, it's Dad."

"I know who you are."

"What?"

"Nothing. What's going on?"

"Bill and I just came back from the buffet."

"Where, Suncoast?"

"No. It was another one. I don't know which one it was. It was . . . I don't know. Anyway, we had a twofer, so we went for breakfast first."

"I thought you didn't waste coupons on breakfast."

"Wait, wait."

"OK. How much was breakfast?"

"It was cheap. Only four bucks, nothing special. but we had a twofer, so it was four bucks for the two of us."

"So you did waste a coupon on that?"

"Let me tell you the beautiful part."

"Beautiful part?"

"We got lunch, too."

"You got lunch? Where?"

"Yeah. We had breakfast about, I guess, around, I don't know, 9:30, and then we ate, bullshit, bullshit, but we noticed that the lunch buffet was starting around 11:00, so we got out of there about 10:30, but we didn't leave. We hung around outside the buffet entrance, in the front, but inside — you know what I'm saying?"

"Yeah, I think so."

"So we waited while they were changing things from breakfast to lunch."

"Yeah, and?"

"They opened and then, we, uh, just slid into lunch."

"You slid into lunch?"

"Yeah, we were standing there and we weren't totally outside the, you know, area, so we walked right in. Nobody stopped us."

"So you ate lunch right after eating breakfast?"

"Yeah, what the hell, right?"

"Right. So, essentially, you got two breakfasts for the price of one, and then you completely cheated them and got two lunches for free, so all in all, you had four meals for the price of one."

"Yeah."

"Were you hungry for lunch 20 minutes after eating breakfast?"

"That's not the point."

"Of course not. You know, Dad, you should use your power for good."

"What's that?"

"Nothing.

"And I won $63 at Crap."

"Craps."

"What?"

"Craps."

"That's what I said."

"You said 'Crap'!"

"Is it Craps or Crap?"

"Craps."

"I call it Crap."

"Then why'd you ask?"

"I like the game. It's fast-moving."

"Weren't you afraid of getting caught at the buffet?"

"Nah, they don't care."

"I think they'd care."

"Nah. So if they stopped us, they stopped us. That's all."

My father fears neither the IRS nor Summerlin casino buffet managers.

As much as he liked buffets, he never understood why there were never enough spoons. He thought it was a conspiracy at worst, a simple cost-cutting measure at best. "See, Ba, the spoon is the most versatile utensil, so that's why people steal them and that's why restaurants don't put them out. I've thought about stealing them, too, when I see them."

"You thought about stealing spoons?"

"Well, they don't put enough out. What am I supposed to do?"

His buffet prowess wasn't always so successful. On one of my sister's trips to Vegas, she and I accompanied him to Bally's, on Las Vegas Boulevard, where he played Crap and we played nickel Keno. We met him at the prescribed time and place; he was smiling broadly. This always meant a big win.

"What happened?" Susan asked, at which point he peeled off a $100 bill and gave it to her, then peeled off another $100 and gave it to me.

"What is this for?" I asked.

"I had a good day. I won $1,100."

"Good for you," I said.

"C'mon," he said, "we'll have lunch. I'm buying."

We walked along the corridor between Bally's and Paris and found a Le Village Buffet, a French buffet. The "Le" makes it art, don't you think?

"You sure you want to go here, Dad?" Susan asked.

"Yeah, yeah."

"It's, like, 28 bucks . . . for lunch," she said. "We really don't have to."

My father had a plan, though.

"Now, look, when we get to the front, when they ask how many, just say there are two of us."

"Won't they know there are three by, you know, looking at us and counting?" I asked.

"Nah, they won't check. Just say two."

"They won't check? They don't have to do much sleuthing here. There are three of us."

"They're not going to check. I've done this a thousand times."

We got to the cashier.

"How many in your party?" the woman asked.

"Two!" my father blurted. "Just two," he said again, as Susan and I looked on.

Inexplicably, the cashier said nothing, as he paid with one of his $100s.

Could this actually work?

Short answer: no.

When we got to the entrance to the actual buffet, the woman who'd be taking us to our seats saw three of us, did a double take, and checked the receipt.

"Sir, you only paid for two here."

"Well, I'm not eating," my father said. "I'm just going to sit."

Oh, that's good, Dad.

"Sir, I can't let you in."

"Really, I'm not hungry. I'm just going to sit."

"Sir, again, I can't let you in. You'll have to pay for another if you want to go in with your party."

"So what do I do?" my father asked, suddenly unaware of buffet protocol.

The woman told him to go back to the cashier.

"Dad, I'll go," I said. "You stay here with Susan."

He peeled out another $100 and handed it to me.

"Don't forget to get the change."

"Your plan was thwarted, Dad, huh?" I said when I returned.

"Ach, what do they want from my life?"

"Apparently just that you pay for all the people coming to a buffet."

"Ach!"

"Dad, I appreciate you buying here."

"I do too," said Susan.

"But next time" — by this time I can't stop laughing — "why don't you give Susan and me $86, instead of $100, and take the $14 from each and cover the buffet."

"You know," he said, "the shrimp here is very good."

"Good."

"You eat shrimp?" he asked me.

"Yes, I eat shrimp," I said.

"Since when?"

"I don't have a date, but yeah."

"You eat shrimp? I didn't know you ate shrimp. When did you come to eat shrimp?"

~

BECAUSE BOTH MY brother and sister have real jobs — and I was (and am) a comedian — I spent more time with my father after my mother died than they did, and it is because of that, since 2004, when he moved to Las Vegas, that I became the unofficial scribe of the life of Jack Friedman.

Some variation of this conversation happened almost weekly.

"How do you live, making the money you make?" he'd ask more than occasionally.

"How?"

"Yeah, how?"

"I live."

"You don't live."

"I live!"

"Nah, you're not living."

"I can come out to see you every few months to plug in your router or printer. If I had a real job, I couldn't do that."

"Yeah, I guess you're right."

By the aughts, I was working six to eight weeks per year at Sin City Comedy, inside the Planet Hollywood casino. The show was an odd combination of topless dancers and comedians; the

dancers would go on first, often in the character of a secretary or
teacher or businesswoman, then more or less strip before leaving
the stage to get into their next outfit and a new "profession" and
return to the stage, where they'd strip again. While they were
changing, drying off, pondering the pathos of their hard-bodied
lives, we comedians would go onstage and perform for 10
minutes, and then they'd return. If it sounds unworkable, sounds
like the worst entertainment sandwich of all time, it was. As a
good friend of mine, Kristi McHugh, said about working such
shows, it was like the audience was looking at us and wondering,
"Why are they talking? Why are they dressed?" Unlike the old
days of the MGM, Bally's, Riviera, Maxim, and Excalibur, Planet
Hollywood did not provide accommodations for the comedians
— nor did they provide, more importantly, unlimited (or any)
access to the buffets, the real disappointment — so when I'd
come to Vegas to work Sin City, I'd stay in my father's second
bedroom, either at the apartment he first rented or eventually at
the house he bought. In the apartment, that bedroom acted as
his office. He was still doing accounting work back then, so we
put a sofa/futon in there for me and other visitors. Often, while
I was still asleep, he'd come into the office at 6:00 or 6:30 a.m. to
tell me, "I'm looking for something. Go back to sleep."

Many years later, after he had moved to Tulsa, I guess he had
a moment to reflect on the time we spent together — or, more
to the point, the time I spent with him.

"Ba," he said on the phone, "I want to thank you for what
you do for me."

My mother and father went with the "Ba" instead of "Barry,"
which, oddly, saved only one syllable.

"What are you talking about? It's what I want to do. I love
you."

"I love you, too, sweetheart. All these years, I don't know
what I'd do without you."

"You don't have to thank me."

"I just want to say I appreciate so what you do, what you've done — the shopping and the whatnot. Susan and Wayne, I know they mean well, but she works and he's sophisticated."

My mother used to talk about my father's inability to give a compliment. Her exact words: "He gives you ice in the wintertime, your father." I was, apparently, the underemployed dolt who kept him in Half-and-Half while my more accomplished siblings pursued fruitful lives.

To listen to my parents talk, and these were both first-generation Americans, was a feast of grammar of syntax. Both Jewish, raised in Jewish homes where Yiddish was spoken freely, they never quite took to the language, which didn't stop them from using it.

When the New York New York casino first opened on Las Vegas Boulevard, my father and I went to take a look. He was not impressed.

"What a hoyzn fabrikant," he said, bringing the Yiddish, as we headed down the escalator to the casino floor.

"What is that?"

"You don't know Yiddish?" he asked.

"Why would I know Yiddish?"

"It means a mess, poorly put together, a terrible design. Hoyzn fabrikant."

"You sure? I don't know Yiddish, but that doesn't sound right."

"Am I sure? Is the Pope Catholic?"

Next time I was back in Tulsa, I was at dinner with my cantor and his wife, who were both friends of mine. We were at a Chinese restaurant — yeah, I know, the jokes write themselves — and I thought I'd show off.

"Alice," I said, "this place is hoyzn fabrikant."

"What are you trying to say, Barry?"

Uh-oh.

"Hoyzn fabrikant. It means 'mess,' right?" I asked, but not confidently.

"Barry, where did you learn Yiddish? Hoyzn fabrikant means 'pants maker.'"

Speaking of things Chinese, I remember one time my father bought a shirt — a "large." But it didn't fit.

"Flo," he said to my mother/his wife, "I don't know why this doesn't fit. It's a large."

"It's a large," she said derisively. "It sat next to a large. For a Chinaman, it's a large."

It's wrong, I know, but, Christ, that still makes me laugh.

ANYWAY, next time I saw my father, I brought it up.

"Hey, by the way, you're wrong about your use of Yiddish. Hoyzn fabrikant does not mean 'mess' — it means 'pants maker.'"

"Where do you get your information?"

"From a cantor's wife, that's where."

"Yeah, well, she doesn't know what she's talking about."

On Tuesdays and Fridays, almost immediately upon arriving in Las Vegas, my father joined two bowling leagues. This was in addition to the Survivors' Group he also joined, whose members also had lost spouses and had relocated to Las Vegas. He referred to those in the group as "the Mob" — not in any Mafia sense, but because there were more than three of them and it was easier than trying to remember all their names. Suncoast Casino, upstairs, had a bowling alley, and since this was the go-to casino anyway for many of them and minutes from where he lived, he looked forward to these two days every week. On his monthly desk calendar, which was essentially empty of any appointment, I could always find Bowling each Tuesday and Friday, the word "Bowling" underlined and circled, as if he might forget. My father and Jeannette — she buried two husbands, you know — shared a locker, which was crammed with two balls and two pairs of shoes. (Years later, as my father's dementia increased, a nurse at his retirement center, and by this time he was living in Tulsa, called one night — I remember I was in the Bahamas, doing comedy — and told me that my father was looking frantically for his bowling ball.)

"He said," the nurse told me, "that it's Monday and he's going to miss his bowling night."

I don't ever remember him bowling on a Monday, but maybe when I was much, much younger, he did. He was a great bowler back when I was in high school. His average was 175 and he used to bowl with a 16-pound ball. He rolled it straight and hard. When his ball would hit the pins, they didn't just scatter, they surrendered. In Vegas, the weight of the ball was down to 12 pounds, he took three steps instead of six, but none of that was important to him. He was in his eighties, he had enough money to live in what he called his "retiring years," and he was in a bowling league that provided soft drinks (one refill) each Tuesday and Friday, if you kept the cup.

"Every day," he told me, in those early days in Vegas, "was a holiday."

When I was out in Vegas, I used to go with him to the Suncoast on Fridays, watch him bowl a little, and then meet some friends for lunch or head back to his house.

"Tell you what, Ba, take the cup, fill it up. You can go back more than once. Tell them you're with the league. Nobody's going to check." He was right. Nobody checked. But he was not about to have someone at the bowling alley concession stand telling him how many refills he was going to get. He was prepared to take Vegas down if he had to.

After Friday bowling, "The Mob" went to dinner. Each member got a turn choosing the place. Since there might be up to 12 of them — spouses, friends, children were also invited — there was much yelling across long tables and they very much looked like a mob. My father always asked me to come along. One Friday, a night it was not my father's to choose, we were headed to Ruby Tuesdays, but I didn't find that out right away.

"Where is this goddamn place?" my father asked as I drove east on Charleston.

"I don't know. You say the place is called Tuesday, Dad? You sure?"

"Yeah. Tuesday — Tuesday something. Tuesday Morning, I think."

"I know it's not that."

"Tuesday something, then, I don't know. I think it's Tuesday Morning."

"It's not Tuesday Morning. Ruby Tuesday, perhaps?"

"No, that's not it!"

"You sure?"

"What's that name again?"

"Ruby Tuesday."

"Yeah, yeah, that's it!"

When we got there, finally, the Mob was hoyzn fabrikant and collectively grumpy. My father had long since stopped talking to Ed, who, my father concluded, not incorrectly, was a racist because Ed wouldn't shut up about blacks and how this country — and this was 2007 — would never elect a "nigger." Ed also wouldn't stop mocking my father's toupee, which was easily mockable, but not by this racist fuck. I'll explain more about the hair later. My father had also had it with Carole, who wouldn't stop trying to correct my father's bowling form. Meanwhile, Velda was there too, having finally dumped Ed's ass, and was now engaged to Tom, the soon-to-be ex-priest. (My father said his church had a "strict obedience" policy about marriage, so he had to leave it, as if other Catholic churches didn't.) Jeannette, my father's girlfriend, whom he was calling every name except "Jeannette," was there, but not sitting next to my father because he refused that night to pick her up. She drove herself.

"What?" he said on the trip to the restaurant that night, "I got to go pick her up, drive to the place, then drive back? It's too much."

"But I'm driving," I said. "I don't mind."

"Yeah, but let it go. You know she's buried two husbands?"

The following week, once again not my father's turn to pick the restaurant, we went to a place called New York Pizza and Pasta in Las Vegas. My father once again refused to pick her up. Again, I drove. Again, he didn't know where we were going.

"Where the hell are you going?" he said as I drove on Jones.

"It's on Jones. I know where it is."

"Why are you on Jones?"

"Because it's on Jones."

"So why you going this way?"

"Because it's this way on Jones. That's why I'm on Jones."

"All right, don't get shook up. I just didn't know why you were on Jones."

Dinner this time went smoothly, or as smoothly as these things can do with seven octogenarians bitching about their aches and pains and bouts with gas and Medicare. As we were leaving, my father saw what looked to be the owner, sitting out front.

"Why do you make your portions so goddamn big?" my father asked the man in khakis and a pink shirt, as we were walking to the car. "Who the hell can eat so much?"

"So take it home," said the guy, the presumed owner, looking up from his New York Post.

"I am taking it home," said my father, "but that's not the point. These meals are enormous. I can't finish it all."

"What do you want me to do, sir? We serve a lot of food. Nobody else complains."

"Nah, I'm not complaining, but it's just a lot of food, that's all. Where do you get a New York Post? Haven't seen one in 50 years."

The following week, I was still in town, as Sin City kept me over, and it was my father's turn to pick.

"Where do you want to go, Ba? You choose."

"Yeah?"

"Yeah."

"Let's go to Ping Pang Pong. It's at the Gold Coast."

"What's it called?"

"Ping Pang Pong."

"Ping Pang who?"

"Pong."

"Pong?"

"Pong. Ping Pang Pong."

"What kind of place is that?"

"German?"

"What?"

"I'm kidding. It's Chinese."

"Yeah?"

"Yeah."

The Mob wasn't impressed. Everyone knew a better Chinese place in town.

My father didn't eat many meals at home, either in the apartment or later when he moved into the house on Tumble Brook. But what he did eat was breakfast. Always the same meal: orange juice, small glass; coffee, decaf mostly, with four packets of Sweet 'n Low and Half-and-Half ("The color should be a soft beige," he would say); and cereal, which he had in a large container, including Chocolate Frosted Flakes, regular corn flakes, and Rice Krispies, which he carefully mixed himself. Like the love of one woman, one cereal could not satisfy this man. As for the decaf, he would also add ice cream as well, or whatever was sweet on the table — like cake or an Oreo or a piece of chocolate, and watch it dissolve. He also didn't like his coffee hot, so he would cool it down with ice cubes, even if the cubes were floating in, say, my Diet Coke. He would reach across the table with his spoon, which had been in his coffee, and then put it into my glass and fetch a cube or two.

"Would you get your spoon out of my glass?"

"I'm just getting ice."

"I know what you're doing. Stop."

"The coffee's too hot — that's all. I'm trying to cool it down."

"But that's your problem — not mine. You can't be putting your spoon in other people's drinks, Dad."

"Why? It's too hot."

"I know it's hot, but this is rude," I said, handing him back his spoon with an ice cube.

"All right, all right, I'm sorry. I was just trying to cool the coffee down, that's all."

The thing about his coffee, invariably through the decades, was it never let him down.

"You know, Ba," he'd say, wherever we were, "they make good coffee here."

"Dad, there are four Sweet 'n Lows, Half-n-Half, chocolate cake, and an ice cube that was floating in a Diet Dr. Pepper — are you even tasting the coffee?"

"What do you know? You're uncivilized."

For a while, he did also eat fruit, but that ended suddenly one day when the fruit turned against him.

"Ba, I'm done with apples," he said one morning, as I walked into the kitchen on Tumble Brook and saw him sitting at the breakfast nook.

"What do you mean? Why apples? What happened?"

"I'm not going to bite down anymore on apples."

"What are you talking about?"

"I broke a tooth."

"Let me see."

"No, it's not that."

"No, that's it. Let me see."

Something wasn't just chipped, it was missing.

"You sure did. Look, it doesn't mean you should stop eating apples. We'll find a dentist for you."

"I don't eat that many anyway."

"Dad, let's get the tooth fixed. You got a dentist here, right?"

"They can't fix it."

"Sure they can."

"No, they can't."

"What are you, a dentist? I'm sure they can fix it. That's what they do. I just wish I knew where it was. There seems to be more than one missing."

"What are they going to do?"

"I don't know. Fix it."

"What's it going to cost me?"

"I don't know. But you have to get it fixed."

"Ach! I don't eat that much."

"Are you kidding me?"

"If it's too much money, I'm not doing it."

"What are you going to do, then, gum your food from now on?"

"Yes!"

"Dad, we'll get it fixed."

"I'm telling you, I'm done with apples."

"Oh, stop it! You could cut up the apple into littler pieces."

"Yeah, but most people, when you think of an apple, you bite down," he said, making a crunching sound and pantomiming the apple.

"So don't be like most people."

"That's not the point."

"It sounds like the point, because you had a large apple that chipped what looks like many teeth."

"I'll eat other fruit, softer fruit. And I know you can eat the apple other ways, but, you know, I'm going to stay away from all hard foods."

"Would you knock it off? You're not going to eat only soft food. Did you lose a tooth or part of your denture? Let me look again."

He smiles so I can see.

"Dad, I think it's a piece of your denture."

"How did that happen?"

"How should I know?"

"The damn apple. Ach, I give up! What do they want from my life?"

"Dad, who? The dental gods? We'll get it fixed."

"I don't know where it is."

"You don't know where the denture is?"

"Did the denture break or did you lose it?"

"I know."

"Well, I don't know."

"I don't know what the hell I did with it. It's around."

"Unless the denture dropped somewhere."

"I just don't know what the hell I did."

"Did you lose it, take it out, or did it break?"

"I . . . uh, I don't know."

"If you lost it, we'll get you a new one. If you broke that one too, we'll fix it."

"Lousy goddamn apple."

"Stop blaming the fruit! We'll get it fixed."

"They're not going to be able to fix it."

AS MY FATHER was close to both the Suncoast and Red Rock casinos, whether at the apartment or the house, he gambled a lot — more than he ever let on. Win or lose, he'd always lie.

"Dad, how'd you do?" I'd ask, meeting him at an agreed-to coffee shop.

"I lost $23."

"Nobody loses $23."

"I did, I did. I lost $23. I don't know, maybe more, maybe less, and then I tipped a few bucks."

"You lost 20 bucks and then tipped three?"

"Yeah, I figured what the hell."

What was good about him being so close, he wouldn't spend more than an hour or so gambling. I know he wouldn't lose more than $100 at a time. The question was: I never knew how many times he lost that much. Most days, for him, especially in the early days in Vegas, he'd drive himself to the gym; early afternoon, he'd go to the casino, eat at the buffet, and then spend the night at home, watching television with an occasional trip back to the casino.

His driving . . . let's put it this way: not the worst, even if he once thought it would be a good idea to take an Ambien one morning at 5:00 because he couldn't sleep and then decided at 8 to take himself to breakfast. He fell asleep driving, totaled his car, and wound up in the ER.

"Then, Ba, I'm lying there," he told me after I came to see him, "the cop drops a ticket on me. The nerve of him!"

He bounced back quickly — he purchased a Honda the next day.

"Why didn't you wait for me?" I asked when he called to tell me.

"He had a nice one, gray, so I thought, what the hell? It was a good deal. I mean, I don't know."

I was with him when he bought the Toyota that he had just wrecked. We were in Mays Landing, a few months after my mom died. At the time, they owned a Buick and a Honda. One morning at breakfast, at around 10:30 — and the time is important — my father announced he thought he should buy a new car and wanted to trade in the two he had. He drove the Honda, I drove the Buick, and off to the dealer we went. A salesman took us to a black Toyota Camry.

"I like black," he said.

"You want to test-drive it?" I asked as the dealer handed me the keys.

"Nah, I've driven enough in my life. You drive it."

I did.

"How was it?" he asked as we pulled back into the dealership.

"Fine."

"All right, let's get it."

Don't remember the exact terms, but he unloaded both cars, got the black Toyota, we stopped for lunch at the Shore Diner, and we were back home by 1:30 that afternoon.

During the eight years my dad lived in Las Vegas, in the apartment near the Red Rock Casino and on Tumble Brook, I always knew when it was time to make a trip out there, even when I wasn't working Sin City.

"Nothing works! Nothing works!" he'd scream into the phone.

"Dad, what happened? What'd you do?"

"I didn't do anything."

"You must have done something. And what doesn't work?"

"Nothing. I turned the stupid thing on and, bingo, nothing!"

"What 'thing'?"

"All of them."

"The computer?"

"The computer, the phone, the printer, the clock — all right, but don't worry about that. Nothing works! Ach! I give up!"

"All right, we'll fix everything. The computer. You gotta tell me, what did you do?"

"I didn't do anything."

"You did nothing? You have to tell me if you did."

"I might have tried to fix the whatchamacallit."

"The what? Oh, boy. And the phone? We're talking on the phone."

"Until I got it to work."

"What about the printer?"

"Nothing. I put it on—"

"—It's always on. Did you turn it off?"

"Turn it off? What, you mean 'off' from before? I don't know what I did. I just tried to adjust—"

"—Adjust? It doesn't need adjusting. You want me to come out?"

"Would ya?"

"Sure."

"I'll pay the carfare."

❀

WHEN HE FIRST MOVED TO the apartment, he bought a bed and some furniture, but was waiting on his clothes and other items to arrive from New Jersey. He called when the movers arrived. While I paid for the option of packing all his things from the condo in Mays Landing, I failed to check the box on the form so that they'd unpack them once he got to Vegas.

"They didn't unpack, Ba."

"You want me to come back?"

"I'll pay the carfare."

He always offered to pay the carfare.

That trip, I remember putting away as much as we could that first night. When I woke, he was sitting in the living room, reading my first book, Road Comic, which apparently he found in one of his boxes.

"What are you doing?" I asked, for my father was not a reader — certainly not of my books.

"You're a good writer, you know that?"

"I am? Thanks, I think."

"No, it's good. What a life you led, but don't think you're the only one."

"What do you mean?"

"You know, the girls, the running around."

"Oh, that — yeah, well, it's kind of embarrassing."

"I did plenty — just so you know. Don't think I didn't."

"I won't think you didn't."

"I did plenty of tumulting."

"Tumulting?"

"Yeah, the running around, the bullshit."

"Tumulting is good."

"You want to know the difference between you and me?" he asked, picking up the book again.

"This should be good."

"All these words in here. I know these words. The difference is you know what order to put them in."

~

He was, as mentioned, still doing accounting work. He was also still doing accounting in pencil and using Bic Wite-Out, which was quaint, unless you were his client. Petar didn't mind. I noticed one return he was doing on Petar's corporate return, which ran 11 pages and encompassed both his medical practice and real-estate holdings, but it had only seven lines filled out.

"Dad," I said, looking it over, "this can't be right."

"What do you mean?"

"I know nothing about taxes, but you only have, like, a few items filled out."

"So Petar gives me the figures, I put them down. How do I know if they're accurate?"

"I'm just saying. This can't be right."

"If it's wrong, the IRS will send him a letter. That's all."

"Pretty cavalier of you."

"What do you want from me? I don't even want to do it anymore."

"Then quit."

"Nah, I make a few bucks. What the hell? Hey, I ever tell you about his wife?"

"Petar's wife? No."

"She wanted to open a nude restaurant."

"What?"

"Yeah, the waiters and waitresses would all be nude. She was wild, that woman. She never did it, at least I don't think she did. She was very nice. I met her."

My father, in his day, was a good accountant. He was not a CPA, even though he told everyone he was. My parents were married 35 years, split up for a year, and then got back together.

"Hey, Dad, how long you and Mom been married?"

"Gross or net?"

As his practice started dwindling, especially after moving from the apartment to the house in Vegas, he decided to discard the years and years of files he had acquired and had stored in his file cabinet. Discarding old returns should be done with a certain amount of caution; preferably a shredder should be involved. If you were my father's client, however, your old tax returns, pay stubs, Social Security payments, medical expenses, investments, etc., still in folders with your name on them, were unceremoniously and haphazardly thrown in a dumpster in a parking lot on South Pavilion Center Drive. As an accountant, even a semiretired one in Vegas with pencils and Bic Wite-Out, my father used to get solicitations from financial organizations and seminars. He discarded most of them, except for the ones that referred to him as a CPA, which he liked and proved, because a label on a mailer that says "Jack Friedman, CPA" validates that you are.

Shopping with my father, actually going to any place of business anywhere with him, even when we were both younger, was always episodic. Once, we walked into a movie theater — this was back when he lived in New Jersey — after having first stopped at Dollar Tree for candy so as not to pay the exorbitant prices at the theater. We arrived at the movie, were inside, having paid admission, as we passed the clerk ripping tickets.

"Sir, sir," he called out, clearly seeing the plastic Dollar Tree bag in my father's hand, filled with Good & Plenty, Raisinets, jelly beans, Snickers, and other assorted items, "you can't take outside candy into the theater."

"It's not candy," my father screamed back, "it's jewelry!"

As I think I mentioned, in the mornings, after moving to Las Vegas, he would go to the gym. Mostly he'd go for the sauna, but he would occasionally do a half hour or so on the treadmill, which for a man in his late seventies and early eighties was quite impressive. He'd strap on his cheap headphones, the kind that come free with a subscription to *Time*, which is where he might have gotten them, and plugged them into a cassette player.

Yeah, cassette.

"Ba," he said once in a call, excitedly, "do you know this group ABBA?"

"Yeah."

"I'm listening to ABBA when I walk. Oh, they're very good."

"Where'd you get an ABBA cassette? Where'd you get a cassette, for that matter?"

"I don't know. I had them."

In New York, he used to have a client who provided management material to JCPenney. Some of this material was on cassette tapes. That's how far back this was. On those tapes were titles like "Management Concepts," "Upselling," "Customer Service." My father simply recorded over those tapes, so he might have, say, a tape titled "Holiday Sales" with the word "ABBA" written over the title in a Sharpie. As it turns out, he wasn't listening to ABBA, he was listening to A-Teens (Abba Teens), which was an ABBA cover band. On some occasions I'd go to the gym with him and see him on the treadmill, bopping along, unconcerned with what he looked like or who was watching. He'd raise his eyebrows and smile, as if to say, "Nu? I'm walking." My father's joy at moments, odd moments — not even close to the seminal ones — was a wonderful thing to see. When he lived in Mays Landing, he once drove me to the airport in Philly. I could tell by the time we got to the terminal that he wasn't feeling well. I didn't want to leave him, but I needed to catch a flight. I told him to wait in the car, and I ran inside and got him a 20-ounce bottle of Coke, two chocolate cupcakes, and a bag of peanuts. Something told me sugar, protein, carbonation, and whatever combustible mix would develop in his esophagus would make him feel better. I handed him the bag through the driver's side window. He looked inside.

"Oh, Barry, thank you. This is perfect. Thank you, sweetheart."

He opened the Coke, took a swig, tore out one of the cupcakes, ate it. He grabbed my hand.

"Perfect. Just perfect."

You would have thought I'd bought him a condo in Boca Raton the way he carried on.

AFTER A FEW YEARS IN VEGAS, though he was still driving, I stopped having him come to McCarran Airport to pick me up.

"Dad, you keep missing the exit," I said to him, seeing the exit as we drove by . . . again.

"Where the hell is it?"

"There?" I pointed to the exit sign that said "Terminal 1."

"What do you mean, 'there'?"

"What do I mean, 'there'? There!" I pointed to it again, as we passed it.

"You know what the problem is?" he asked.

"What's the problem?"

"They keep moving these goddamn roads."

"I don't think they're moving the roads."

"Then why do they make it so difficult? They got a thousand roads here."

"By the way, we have to get your brakes fixed."

"What do you mean?"

"The brakes. They sound like a dentist's drill. Can't you hear them?"

"What am I listening for?"

"There . . . that. That's metal on metal."

"Nah, that's just the sound of the tires on the road."

IT WAS a few months after my bar mitzvah. My family —
brother, sister, mother, and father — were living in Greenlawn,
New York, in a four-bedroom house on the North Shore of Long
Island. It was a house my parents bought in 1965 for $23,000. My
father told me that the mortgage was $115 per month, which was
probably why a man, such as my father, could make $20,000 and
provide for a family of five. When they closed on the house, my
parents got the loan documents and discovered the payments
were not going to be $105, as they had been promised, but the
aforementioned $115. ("Ba, it was such a big deal, that 10 bucks,
we nearly backed out of the house.") That house, incidentally, 35
years later, long after it had many other owners, sold for
$700,000.

Anyway, getting back to the story, it was early one day, I
wasn't yet up for school, and my father appeared at my door,
something he almost never did.

He had hair.

Before then, he wasn't bald, but his hair was definitely thin-
ning, and now he definitely had hair.

"What do you think?" he asked as he stood there.

I squinted with one eye. "That looks good, Dad."

It did, too.

"Yeah?"

"Yeah."

"All right. Have a good day." He walked downstairs.

And now the toupee story.

That first toupee, I came to discover, cost him $300, a huge
amount of money for a hairpiece back then, the mid-1970s.
Evidently, he had gone to a men's salon in New York City and
had one fitted for his head. It looked as good as these things can
look. It was the first and last time he would ever go to a salon

and spend that kind of money. As the years went on, first on Long Island and then in Toms River, New Jersey, where he and my mother moved, and then in Mays Landing, my father would spend less and less money on them. Thing I noticed was, the cheaper the piece, the thicker they were.

"Dad, nobody has hair that thick," I told him once.

"I do."

"You do realize they look awful. Everyone knows you're wearing a toupee."

"You're the only one who can tell I'm wearing one."

"Stevie Wonder can tell you're wearing one."

He never took it off, not at night to sleep, not when he was showering. He used to have hair-bonding glue, which he used for years before the glue, too, was more than he was willing to spend. By then, the pieces, still thick, were more like elastic wigs that would cup around his head. They weren't like wigs — that's exactly what they were. He bought wigs, wiglets, hairpieces — whatever euphemisms were being used — from a company called Paula Young. They'd come in boxes that he'd put on his head and style (cut with a dull scissors) while he faced a mirror. When a mirror wasn't around, he did it free-hand, meaning that the cut, as you would imagine, would often go awry. There could be an inverted V up the back of his neck. He looked at times like he was an alien in a world where some existed. They would all have the V up the back of the neck, which is how they would recognize each other. When such an imperfection was noticed by him, and bothered him, he would take the cut up even higher and try to straighten it out; hence his hairpiece might only cover half the back of his head. Some of the pieces had built-in tousles, some had parts, some did not. There were blond ones, red ones, light-brown ones, dark-brown ones, and one salt-and-pepper. Often when he'd get a new piece, it would come on you fast and unannounced, not unlike turning a corner in Paris and having the Eiffel Tower seemingly appear out of nowhere. At times there was more than one piece lying around, so it was reminiscent of the "Tribble" episode on Star Trek where they just started multiplying. If he spent more than $59, Paula Young would provide free shipping. Spending $59 meant he'd have to buy two at a time, which he would do. Years later, when my brother and I cleaned out his garage in Las Vegas, prior to the move to Tulsa, we found boxes of hair in his suitcase, boxes of hair in old tennis bags, boxes of hair in old chests of drawers. These boxes had names . . . Ashlee, Calla, Ricki. My father had them all.

"You'd look a lot better," I used to say to him, "if you just removed it. You're in your eighties, nobody is expecting you to have hair — and certainly not this much hair."

"It makes me feel better. What can I tell you?"

"I just don't want people laughing at you."

"What do I care?"

"But you do care. The same vanity that makes you wear them is the same vanity that would destroy you if you thought that people were laughing at you because of them. How about when we move to Tulsa, you take them off?"

"Ahh, why does it bother you?"

"Because you're a better-looking man without it."

I never knew why it bothered me so much.

One morning and early afternoon, after we all slid into a lunch buffet — my father, Bill, Bill's wife, and I — we went back to Bill's, where Bill sat him down in his garage on a folding chair.

"Jack, I'm going to cut your hair."

"It's not my real hair, you know," my father said.

"I know, Jack."

"We all know, Dad."

I was there to witness this haircut. God is good.

Bill was not a barber, not even close. He was, as mentioned, a retired cop from Indiana, but he, too, didn't like the snickering he'd hear when people would point out his friend's toupees, and because Bill could see the back of my father's head, he decided he was going to "even things out."

And he did.

Fake toupee hair littered Bill's garage floor. He pulled out the Shop-Vac to clean up.

My father's toupee looked terrible, but no longer comical.

On the short drive back to my father's house on Tumble Brook — Sun City in Las Vegas is its own universe, and one never has to leave — I said, "That was nice of Bill."

"What? You mean the hair?"

"Yes, I mean the hair."

"Yeah, he fixed it. But I cut it, too."

"I know. You do a shitty job, too. That's why Bill fixed it."

"I do fine. You don't know."

"Dad, look, you buy hair that comes in a box. What does that tell you? It can't possibly look good."

"What do you want me to do?" he asked. "That's the way it comes."

Go ahead. You argue with that kind of logic.

When the piece finally came off — and I'm skipping ahead a decade or more — my father, my girlfriend, Melissa, and I were sitting in my dining room in Tulsa, eating Chinese takeout. I knew a woman at the restaurant who made my father his favorite, shrimp egg foo young.

"You know what's good about this, Ba," he said, picking up one of the egg omelets, "is they put the shrimp inside the, you know, the thing, and they don't just lay the shrimp on top, like a lot of other places. You know what I'm saying?"

"I do."

"But why do they give you so goddamn much?"

"Jack," Melissa said, pointing to his toupee and watching him futz with it, "why don't you just take it off already? You really will look better."

And just like that, he did. Right there over the fried rice and dumplings and shrimp egg foo young. He took it off, held it in front of him in an "Alas, poor Yorick" tableau. We recorded him talking to it.

"You're through, nobody wants you anymore. You have had a good life, but that's it. Goodbye and good luck."

It was beautiful. An hour later I bought him a hat at Target.

The pieces were off his head, but not gone. Once in a great

while, he'd come to the door of his apartment in Tulsa — by this time he was living in a retirement center, Zarrow Pointe in Tulsa, a place he called the "Hebrew Home" — and he'd be wearing a piece. After that night of Chinese food, I threw out all the pieces he had, even the ones he wanted to keep, the ones he called "spares."

I thought I did, anyway.

"The hell is on your head?" I asked after meeting him at dinner one night in the dining room.

"I just found it. Thought I'd wear it around."

"Wear it around?"

"I just put it on, that's all."

"I can see that."

"I don't wear it all the time."

"The hell is wrong with you? Take it off. It's dusty and doesn't fit."

"You don't know what you're talking about. I'm just wearing it, that's all."

"What kind of answer is that? Dad, listen to me: It doesn't fit. It really does look awful, and everyone here knows it's fake. You're not fooling anyone."

"They don't know."

"They know, trust me."

"How do they know?"

"They see you every fucking day."

"Ach!"

"What does that mean? Take it off, please."

"No."

"Dad, please. It really does look awful."

"I don't wear it out."

"You're out now."

"I mean out out — not here."

"When do you wear it?"

"Just around the apartment."

"Well, you're out of the apartment now."

Julie, a friend who works at Zarrow, happened to be in the dining room.

"Julie, help me out here," I begged.

"Oh, Jack. You look so much better without it."

"What?"

"The hairpiece. Take it off."

"He told you to say that, didn't he?"

On the way home that night, I called my sister.

"There was one on his head."

"Do something."

"I'm trying."

"I thought you said you got them all."

"I thought I did too."

"Fuck!"

"I know."

"What are they, growing?"

"I think so."

On two occasions at his apartment, I found toupees in a sock drawer, a drawer that held a heating pad — maybe they were growing — and I quickly scooped them up and shoved them into my pocket. He never saw, or never noticed, that I left his apartment with Ashlee in my pocket. Still, there were conversations like this:

"Say, Ba, where's my hair?"

"Your hair? You haven't had any for 50 years."

"What are you talking about? I just lost it."

"Dad, you have been wearing toupees for the last four decades."

"I still wear them once in a while. You don't know."

Staying with that part of his anatomy, it was getting increasingly obvious as the years progressed that a perfect storm was developing. He couldn't hear, didn't listen, had no short-term memory, and ultimately didn't care what was being said to him. The hearing aids, which started with ones he picked up at Best Buy for $15— there was just one of them, powered by a AAA battery — eventually morphed into actual aids, though he called them "plugs" or "earrings," from the Veterans Administration.

"Why are you telling me to wear these things? I hear fine."

"No, you don't."

"What?"

"Exactly."

"My hearing is fine."

"What do these plugs do exactly, anyway?"

"They enhance your hearing."

"I can hear what you're saying. I'm telling you I don't need them."

"No, you can't."

"What?"

"What are we, doing a routine here?"

"What?"

"Dad, you need the hearing aids, but they only work if you wear them," I said, noticing he wasn't wearing them.

"I wear them."

"But you're not now."

"I take them off when I leave the apartment."

"But that's when you need them — when you're around other people."

"I know, I know. But I want to give my ears a rest."

"Are your ears tired?"

"Well, you know."

"Please wear them."

"All right, all right, but I don't really need them."

On one trip, about a decade ago, I went to see him in Vegas and noticed what looked to be another hearing device, still in a package, re-taped, on his desk, and clearly bought over the counter.

"You bought another one of these things?"

"I don't know how to work the stupid thing."

"Even if you did, it won't work. It's only for one ear."

"The bad ear."

"You don't have a bad ear."

"I don't?"

"No. You have two bad ears. And why would you buy only one anyway?"

"It was only 15 bucks."

His first pair of legitimate hearing aids was $1,500. During the exam, it was discovered he had 70 percent hearing loss in one ear and 50 percent loss in the other.

"Well, I was in the war," he told the audiologist. "You think I might have lost my hearing there?"

"Dad," I interrupted, "you didn't lose your hearing in the war."

"I'm not suggesting I did."

"You literally just suggested that."

"I have a Purple Heart, you know?" he said to the audiologist.

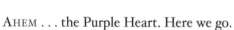

AHEM . . . the Purple Heart. Here we go.

My father enlisted in the Army in 1944. He was 18, maybe a little younger. Seventy years later, I found a picture of him in uniform, full head of hair, scared, brave, and everything in between. I showed it to him.

"Where did you get this?" he asked.

"I don't know. What do you think?"

He took a long look.

"Imagine, Ba, this is who they sent to win the war."

I sent the picture to Charlie Pierce at Esquire, a good friend, whose father was stationed on a sub in the Mediterranean — my dad was sent to the Philippines — and shared with Charlie my dad's comment about who the government had at its disposal to save what Charlie called "the whole damn thing."

"They all felt that way," Charlie wrote back, "and they did it anyway."

The Purple Heart would play an outsize role in the life of Jack Friedman, whether it was his or not.

The story through the years kept changing. My father keeps changing it. The part about him enlisting in the Army in 1944 is true — maybe the only part. Here's the version he likes most: He was being sent to Europe, but just as he was boarding the ship, some officer yelled, "Friedman!" and he was told to get off the boat. His mother, my grandmother, was dying, this officer told him, and my father was granted a two-week furlough. When he got back to Brooklyn, he discovered she had made it up to prevent him from going to Europe, or, as she pronounced it, "Euop." Riva Friedman, who had a son stationed in England at the time and another one at a base in North Carolina, simply didn't want her youngest son, my father, to go into battle. A wonderful story, right? Yeah, except my cousin, the son of the father who was stationed in North Carolina, said our grand-mother would never have taken energy away from her standing poker game to come up with such a scheme. Anyway, after the two weeks were over, the Army shipped my father to the Philip-pines with the First Cavalry, which my father made clear through the decades did not mean he ever rode a horse into battle — not that anyone ever thought he did. One day, in battle (and not on a horse), to hear my father tell it, outside Manila, his command was putting up a bridge. He was holding a large cement block to aid that effort when the Japanese started shelling.

"Drop what you're doing and run for cover!" he said the sergeant yelled.

Which my father did, but he dropped the block of cement on his foot, and then started running.

"You're running the wrong way!" my father says is the last thing he heard from the sergeant before he passed out but after he heard kaboom. (My father has made the kaboom sound for as long as I've known him.)

He said upon waking, he looked down, took off his boot, and saw a nail protruding from his toenail and then passed out, presumably again. One of the nails inside the boulder — I don't know how they got there — dislodged itself from the cement block and then made its way through my father's toenail. Next thing he says he remembers is waking up in a mobile Army hospital . . . in Tokyo.

"I get up and I don't know where the hell I am. I don't know from nothing. But I have to go to the bathroom. And when I come back, there's a Purple Heart on my bed."

Apparently, it was customary that Army personnel would walk the halls of these mobile hospitals, tossing Purple Hearts on the beds of wounded soldiers; so it is possible my father in fact would have gotten one for his injury; however, when I actually saw the Purple Heart, there was nothing engraved on it — and usually one will find the words "For Military Merit." Further, after finding a copy of his Honorable Discharge (Private First Class, Troop B, 8th Engineering Squadron, 1st Cavalry Regiment) — years after hearing the story about the bathroom trip and the tossed award — I noticed he had a Good Conduct medal, an Army Occupation medal, an Asiatic-Pacific Theater ribbon, and a World War II Victory ribbon. There was no mention of the Purple Heart.

"Dad, tell me the Purple Heart story again," I asked him one day at breakfast at the Bagel Cafe in Las Vegas.

"I get back from the bathroom and there's a Purple Heart on my bed. I mean, I think it was my bed. Who can remember?"

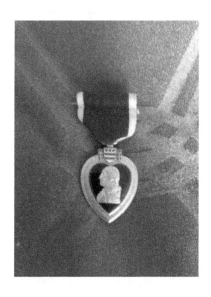

I felt like he had dropped that cement boulder on my head.

"What do you mean, you can't remember?"

"I was groggy."

"So you don't know what bed you were in?"

"There was a lot of beds."

"So you could have gone back to someone else's bed?"

"I don't know. It was, like, 100 years ago."

"Dad, you know, it's possible your Purple Heart may not belong to you."

"What are you talking about?"

"You might have gone back to someone else's bed and it was his Purple Heart lying on the pillow."

"Nah."

"I'm just saying it's possible. There's no record of you having a Purple Heart in your discharge papers."

"They didn't write all that down."

"They didn't?"

"No."

"What about my injuries?" he insisted.

"You broke a toenail."

"It never grew back right."

"Granted. Thank you for your service."

"What about my knee?"

"What about your knee?"

"It hurts."

"You're 90. It doesn't hurt because of a war injury."

"And my hearing?"

"You're going to blame that on the war, too?"

"The shelling was loud."

"Dad, the Purple Heart, seriously, might not be yours."

"Ah, come on!"

"I'm just saying," I said.

"Let it go."

"Let it go?"

"Yeah, let it go. Who can remember?"

On the way home, I called my sister to tell her the news. She did some further checking and again couldn't find any record of him receiving a Purple Heart. Another wrinkle to the story: There was a fire at the National Personnel Records Center (NPRC) in St. Louis in 1973 that destroyed 16-18 million Official Military Personnel Files (OMPF) documenting the service history of former military personnel discharged from 1912 to 1964. It's entirely possible there was no longer a record of his Purple Heart, even if there had been.

"So I called Dad," my sister told me days later, "and said, 'We need to find out about this Purple Heart — whether it's yours or not.' "

"What did he tell you?" I asked.

"He said, 'Just let it go.' "

"That's what he told me. Sue, your father stole some guy's Purple Heart."

"Why is he my father when he steals things?"

"I'm not claiming him. Hey, what if the guy is alive? He could be sitting with his son at, I don't know, a Panera and bitching, 'That son of a bitch Friedman stole my Purple Heart right off my fucking bed. I know it. I went up to take a leak and I came back and it was gone. That son of a bitch!' and I can imagine his son telling him, 'It's been 70 years, Dad. Let it go.' "

"Dad, I heard you talked to Susan about the Purple Heart."

"Yeah, what about it?"

"She says she can't find the paperwork either."

"Nobody cares about the paperwork, Ba. They just want to see the medal."

After arriving in Las Vegas — quickly after arriving — my father met Jeannette.

"No sex, Barry, just friends," he said, "but I think she wants more."

Still, I found condoms in his dresser — and he was 87 at the time — so he hadn't completely given up on the concept.

One day, my father and Jeannette and I decided to go to the

border town of Primm, Nevada. Jeannette invited her friend Carole — not Carole from the group, another Carole.

"Carole's husband was killed in a robbery," my father told me on the way to Jeannette's trailer.

"That's awful!"

"Yeah, but don't say anything."

"Why would you think I'd bring that up? And why would you even tell me that story so now that's all I can think about?"

"And you know Jeannette's buried two husbands? She never even had sex with the second one."

"How much information do you think I need here? And you told me both those stories."

As my father's car needed the brakes fixed — yeah, he finally listened to me — and because Jeannette could drive, but her car was small and she didn't drive well at night, Carole offered the use of her car, if I would drive. Moreover, she proposed, we could either fill her car with gas or buy her lunch at the buffet in Primm. We chose the gas. Then we got in the car. Her tank was about a quarter filled. The drive from Vegas to Primm is about 85 miles. We were going to get screwed on the deal.

"We can just fill up on the way back," she said.

Of course we can, yes.

My father sat in the front seat with me. From the back, I overheard Carole tell Jeannette she had a problem with Millie. I couldn't resist.

"What's the matter with Millie?" I asked.

"First off," Carole said, "she never stops telling jokes, but the big thing: She wears dresses that don't cover her heinie."

"What a hussy!" I said.

At around 1 p.m. we arrived in Primm — Carole's car still had enough gas to make it home — and we decided to eat at Miss Ashley's Boarding House Buffet, which was offering a special Sunday buffet for $14.95. Carole and Jeannette walked in front of us. We stopped at the cashier.

"Dad, looks like we're paying for Carole."

"Where's the meat on this chicken?" my father asked, poking around on his plate after we sat.

"I don't know," I said, looking at it.

"And margarine they have, not butter! This place is uncivilized."

"Crap" did not go well. "You can't win at this goddamn place," my father said when I found him.

We then headed back to Vegas. Before we got back to Jean-nette's, Carole directed me to her favorite gas station, where she, of course, got premium. I thought the buffet was in lieu of gas. Carole expected it to be in addition to.

The defeat left me cold.

That evening on the way back to my father's, he said to me, "We bought her lunch and filled up her car? This is the last time we're taking her out. And there was no chicken on that bone."

MY FATHER'S BROTHER, my Uncle Leo, who is four years older than my father, lives in Delray Beach, Florida, and has for the past 40 years with his wife, my Aunt Marilyn. They have been married 72 years, and for the past few years we have been going down together to see them. I'm not sure how close my father and Leo were growing up, but I'm pretty sure they spent more time together on these trips than they had since they were boys growing up in Brooklyn. When your father and uncle and aunt are in their nineties, you don't know how many more chances they're all going to have to get together.

First time we went down to visit, Leo promised to take us to a great Italian place. I thought it was going to be wonderful, figuring he would know from good Italian food. I had imagined some little Italian guy — and I don't know why I assumed he would be little — who had owned a restaurant in Manhattan or Brooklyn and decided at some point to close it up north and relocate to this part of Florida and open a new place for all the retirees who were dissatisfied by chain Italian restaurants like Macaroni Grill.

"Pull in here," Leo said from the back seat.

It was a parking lot for, you guessed it, Macaroni Grill. Surely, I thought, Luigi's or Mario's or Sol's was in a shopping center in another part of the strip.

Nope. This was it.

"Leo, you're joking, right? Please tell me you're joking."

"No, it's very good."

"No, it's not very good. Besides, we have Macaroni Grills in Tulsa."

"It'll be fine."

It wasn't fine. Of course it wasn't fine. But that wasn't important. After the meal, Leo, who was six feet two and 240, was standing with my father by the restaurant's wall of wine.

"Jackie, it's good to see you."

Only my mother and Leo called him that.

"You, too, Leo."

Leo then hugged my father and lifted him off the ground.

What an odd, wonderful moment that was.

That year, Marilyn and Leo were, in fact, celebrating their 72nd anniversary.

"Marilyn, you've been married 72 years?"

"Yeah," she said dryly. I think the Miami Heat had just lost, so she was in a bad mood. "Seventy-two years. Oy!"

"Happily married?" I asked, smiling.

"Barry, the first 70 years were wonderful, but the last two, you can have 'em."

I thought that was hilarious.

"Marilyn, really, you've really crunched those numbers to that extent."

Leo and Marilyn's place was only about 30 minutes from Marjory Stoneman Douglas High School in Parkland, Florida. I bring it up because my Uncle Leo, a Jewish postman from Brooklyn, who because of an injury delivering mail — the details are neither important nor known — retired to Florida with the help of a loan from the third brother, Hyman, and became an avid gun collector and shooter. He entered contests, made his own bullets in the garage, read magazines about guns and weapons. He was a rarity: a New York Jewish liberal member of the National Rifle Association. As the years went on, he also developed macular degeneration; still, long after he stopped driving because of his vision, he still shot pistols, made his own bullets, and went to the range.

Dana Loesch, the NRA's prominent spokeswoman, is a pustule; Uncle Leo is an old man who hugs his younger brother at Macaroni Grill and hunches over a workbench full of ingots most days. Loesch and Leo belonged to the same organization. I don't know what you do with that. You want someone with Leo's respect for and knowledge of weapons to be packing when someone breaks into your house at three in the morning; you just don't want him, at 95, to be that person — being ostensibly blind and all. On a number of visits, I asked multiple times about his membership in the NRA.

"Barry," he'd say, "this is the story," which is how he began most stories, by announcing he was about to announce a story. The story, however, I could never follow, but it had something to do with the insurance the NRA provides to gun ranges and shooters. With membership, you also get your choice of maga-zine, membership cards, and decals, all of which Leo had no use for — but there was the insurance he, or the range, had to carry. That's why he was a member. Again, I never quite got it, but this was a man who had licorice, jelly beans, and orange slices waiting for me each time I came to visit, so it wasn't important that I follow the logic. This was a good man. Marilyn, however, was easier to follow: She hated the NRA.

"They're always calling for money," she told me once. "Ach, enough already! How much already?"

"So hang up the phone, Marilyn," Leo would bark. "Why do you talk to them?"

"Because, Leo!" she'd bark back without finishing her thought.

Seventy-two years of marriage, I imagine, you've finished all your thoughts.

Marilyn and Leo, because of their respective hearing losses — his worse than hers — were always screaming at one another, not always out of anger. Even when having sweet moments, such as they were. I once saw her try to help him put his hearing aids in.

"Where the hell are you putting them?" he asked, squirming.

"In your ass! Where do you think I'm putting them?"

"You don't know what you're doing."

"You want me to help you, Leo, or not?"

"Fine. Do whatever you want."

"Can you hear?"

"I can't hear anything. You're doing it wrong, I'm trying to tell you."

"Wrong? I'm putting them in your ears. How are they wrong?"

"I don't know, but they're wrong."

"Well, I don't know, Leo."

"I'm telling you that you're putting them in wrong."

"Then you put them in."

"Leave me alone. I'll put them in."

"Fine," she said. Then she looked at me and added, "Nu?"

A tender moment, don't you think?

On those mornings after Leo shot guns at ranges, he'd go to the club in the community center. It wasn't a country club per se, but close enough for old Jews on a pension. The place had great egg salad sandwiches. My father never went to the range with him, nor did I, but we used to join him and Marilyn at the club and have lunch. We'd then return to their house and spend the rest of the afternoon talking about who died and where we should go to dinner.

"Who died, again?" my father would ask.

"Srul!" Leo would say.

"Srul" is short for "Israel," which some Jewish parents named their sons.

"Who?"

"Srul!" Marilyn would scream.

"Oh, yeah, yeah," my father'd say, "I remember. When did he die?"

"Who knows when he died? I don't know when he died," said Leo. "Years back, but here's the story."

"But when did he die?" my father asked, apparently forgetting he just asked.

"We don't know, Jack!" Marilyn screamed.

"Why are you screaming?" Leo asked.

"He can't hear," she said, pointing to my father.

"So he can't hear."

"Who can't hear?" my father asked, adding, "You know Bernie Newman died, too."

"We know. You told us yesterday," Marilyn said.

"How did he die?" my father asked, even though he brought it up.

"I don't know," Marilyn said, "just like yesterday, when you told me, I didn't know."

"He was a cousin," my father said.

"I know he was a cousin. He was Leo's cousin, too."

"How did he die?" my father asked.

"I DON'T KNOW!"

"I mean, that's what I heard."

"Yeah, Bernie died," Leo said calmly.

"Which Bernie?" my father asked. "Schechter or Newman?"

"They both died," Leo said.

"Bernie died, too? I mean, Schechter?" my father asked. "When did he die? What? Am I the only one left?"

"Well, Dad, to be accurate," I chimed in, "Leo and Marilyn are still here too."

"Yeah," he said with a laugh. "I guess you're right."

Conversations like this went on every afternoon we were there. Bernie Newman, though, was someone who was much more important to my father in death than he was in life, even though they were — he was right — first cousins and grew up together. Thing is, they hadn't spoken in 40 years. There was also a third Bernie, in addition to Schechter, and that was Bernie Metz, who was married to Lylah, and accused my father of cheating at pinochle.

"What a piece of work that Bernie was," my father said on the way back to our hotel that night. "I heard he and Lylah both died, too. You don't remember Bernie Newman?"

"Why would I remember him? He was your cousin — not mine."

"That's right," my father said, "this was before your time. You weren't produced yet."

My grandmother Riva, my father's mother, had 11 brothers and sisters — or so my father sometimes maintains.

Molly, one of her older sisters, who was married to Joe, or maybe it was Max, was the mother of Bernie. Growing up, they belonged to a social organization called OFAL (One for All). Bernie's death, if it happened, how it happened, when it happened, was inexplicably on my father's mind for decades. Even after I moved my father to Tulsa and, say, I was picking him up at his apartment, he'd get in the car, and the matter of Bernie's demise would come up.

"Did Bernie Newman die?" he'd ask as he climbed in.
"That's your first question?"
"No. I'm just curious."
"Yes."
"He did?"
"You told me he did."

"I told you that?"

"Yes."

"I heard that. Someone told me."

"Someone?"

"Yeah, I was talking to someone, so I guess he died, but I don't know."

"You don't know who told you?"

"Well, I think he died, but I don't know. I wonder how he died. He was a few months older than me."

"There's probably your answer right there."

"I should find out."

"Call Ida."

"Ida? She's not family?"

"But she married into family."

"She married Max Meltzer, another cousin."

"There were a lot of Maxes in the family, weren't there?"

"Well, there was Max Meltzer, who we called Red, and Jerry Parker, who married Pitsy."

"Was he called Max, too?"

"Jerry? No."

"OK, I guess we're done with the Maxes in the family."

Pitsy was Selma's nickname because she was tiny. Selma was also Bernie's sister. There was another Selma, she lived in the Bronx, who was also tiny, but only the Brooklyn Selma got the nickname.

"Wait. Hold on. Let's get back to Bernie Newman. I really do think Ida would know, Dad, and it's clearly on your mind."

"Her son died, you know?"

"Ida's son?"

"Yeah. Dropped dead walking across the street. I met him once in New York. Nice guy. Yeah, I should call her. She would know. You never met Bernie, did you?"

"No, I met Ida."

"When did you meet Ida?"

"Every time we go down to Florida, we see Ida."

Marilyn and Leo were not crazy about Ida, who lived near Delray, but in a swankier community.

"She is not a well woman," Marilyn said on the way to dinner one time. "She had the stroke and God knows what else. We don't really like her. We don't see her unless you come to visit. Leo has no use for her."

Usually after dinner with Leo and Marilyn, my father and I would go to one of the two casinos in the area — Seminole Casino Coconut Creek or the Hollywood Seminole Hard Rock.

"A woman came up to me," he said one night after gambling. "And she was giving me the eye."

"Was she a hooker?"

"What do you mean?"

"A hooker."

"A hooker?"

"A hooker."

"A hooker?"

"This could go on for a while. Yes, a hooker. What did she want?"

"Who?"

"The hooker."

"Nothing. She was just giving me the eye. She complimented me on the way I was playing."

"You're a nickel player and she was complimenting you?"

"Yeah!"

"She likes the high-rollers, clearly."

"What?"

"Nothing."

"Say, Ba, do they really charge for parking here?" he said as we were leaving the casino one night.

"Yes."

"The nerve of them."

On one trip to Florida, my father and I drove about 45 miles north, to Palm Beach Gardens, to visit his old friend Marvin Kraftchin, who, according to my father, had two claims to fame:

Marvin was evidently an excellent second baseman — "wiry" is the word my father used — and Marvin Kraftchin, my father also proclaimed, was the only Marvin Kraftchin in the United States.

"Go ahead, look it up. You won't find another one."

I did and I didn't.

We arrived, sat in Marvin's living room, where he and my father reminisced about the old days and, of course, who had died.

"George died? When did George die?" my father asked.

"Years ago."

"You didn't know George," my father said to me. "He was a good-looking guy. Very conceited. He became a doctor. Did you know George?"

"No, Dad, I didn't know George."

"But he died. What about his older brother?" my father asked.

"Dead," said Marvin.

"And his wife?"

"She died."

"She died?"

"Yeah."

"Wow-we-wow. And George's parents?"

"Died."

Marvin invited us to his not-quite country club for lunch, which was very much like Leo's not-quite country club, but there's something about these places and their egg salad sandwiches. Truly fabulous egg-to-mayonnaise ratio. When we returned to Marvin's after lunch, he told us about being a poll worker during the 2000 election — this was Palm Beach County, remember; hanging chads and all — and being threatened by Republican National Committee personnel in the days after the election if he continued with the recount that was underway.

"These guys came in," Marvin said, "as we were counting ballots and told us to stop. We had no idea who they were, but they were all in suits and they were dead serious. Scared the hell out of us. It was the last time I worked on an election."

Worse, my family, I'm convinced, handed that election to George W. Bush.

As you probably remember, the election turned on the inability of voters in Palm Beach County to distinguish on the butterfly ballot between Pat Buchanan, who was running as an Independent and was an anti-Semite, and Al Gore, the Democrat, who wasn't. The butterfly ballots were more complicated than they needed to be, but still not that difficult to figure out. Buchanan's proportion of the vote on Election Day ballots in Palm Beach County was the most anomalous excess of votes for him anywhere in the country. Bush won the state, as it turned out, by 537 votes, giving him the election. He received more than 2,000 votes in Palm Beach County, a place filled with thousands of thousands of Jews like Marvin Kraftchin and Leo and Marilyn Friedman. Anyway, later that week, Leo, Marilyn, and their son Michael and his family; my father and I; Ida and Ida's new boyfriend (she always had new ones); Jerry Parker and Pitsy; and others whose names I never got went to Ben's Kosher Delicatessen in Boca Raton. Jews go to Ben's in Boca with the same respect and passion with which Muslims head to Mecca for the hajj. During the meal, I brought up the erroneous votes for Buchanan.

There were about 15 at the table — seven of them, after hearing news in the days that followed about the problems with the butterfly ballots, were shocked to learn they had mistakenly voted for Buchanan. It's not an overstatement, then — if you're wondering how we got stuck with George W. Bush, Republican philosophy on governance, all the way up to Donald Trump — to say that I have the answer. The people sitting at Ben's Deli that night, eating tongue sandwiches and knishes, that's how. The Friedmans. My people did that for America.

BACK IN LAS VEGAS after this trip, one Sunday afternoon we went to Carole's, the original, for a barbecue. My father always invited me to every event "the Mob" had. I was very much an intruder, but he must have enjoyed my company, because there was never any question that I'd join him, even when I told him I'd be fine hanging out by myself. He would hear none of it.

"Come, come. They like you."

"You want me to come? You sure?"

"Yeah, yeah. We'll schmooze around. Bullshit, bullshit."

On this particular Sunday, because they were all in their eighties, Carole talked of her elbow surgery, others talked of bladder problems, heart issues, cramps, incontinence, and then Lou, a practicing Catholic and former real-estate guy, told a great story about a woman he met online.

"I go to visit her and she's very nice, a little heavier than I thought, but OK. I notice, though, her apartment is a bit messy. She's a bit of a slob."

"It's her apartment," my father said, "it's your business?"

"It surprised me," Lou said. "Anyway, so we're getting along all right, but Sunday comes along and I want to go to church. Well, she doesn't want to go, so I tell her I'm going to go without her."

"You told her you were going to church alone?" I asked.

"Yeah."

"How did that go over?"

"Well, she starts getting frisky and she wants to have sex, and I told her no. So we have a big fight and I tell her to take me to the airport and I'm going home. By the time we get to the airport, she's crying and she says, 'Lou, c'mon, we had an argument. It was nothing.' I tell her, 'No, I'm going home.'"

"Jesus, Lou, really?"

"Yes! So then she says, 'Lou, I know you love me, I know it in my heart.'"

"What did you say to that?"

"I told her that I swore on my dead wife's grave I didn't love her."

"You brought up your dead wife?"

"I did."

"There's no coming back from that, you know."

Carole brought up her hatred of socialism.

"I don't trust government in my medicine cabinet."

"You don't?" I asked. "Carole, not to put a damper on the barbecue, but everyone at this table would be dead without socialized medicine."

"We paid in," she said.

"Not enough."

"What do you mean, not enough?"

I had this statistic ready.

"Carole, look, Medicare was started in the mid-60s, you all paid into the system at most 25 years. The Medicare tax was less than one percent when it started, but, all right, let's call it one percent. So if you made $100,000, which you didn't, and paid in for 25 years at that rate, which you didn't, you would have paid $25,000 into the system — again, which you didn't. But even if you did, your elbow surgery you just had ate up most of that. You're out of money. The point here is that I think society should take care of you. We should make it so you can go to the doctor four times a week, as much as you want, and then bitch about all your aches and pains for many, many years. I think it's good we take care of the people at this table. But show some appreciation. Pay it forward, for Chrissakes!"

"Who invited you?" Carole said, laughing.

"Dad, this is where you come in."

"I've never seen this man before," he said, pointing to me

Ivan then began talking about gun ownership.

"Nobody is taking my gun."

"Nobody wants your gun, Ivan," I said. "Carole is never going to invite me back — but we have too many guns in this country."

"I think people should be allowed to protect themselves. People here at this table."

"You should be able to. You can. You know how to handle them. But you really want my father having a gun? Look at him."

At the moment he was trying to open up a new bottle of ketchup.

"I don't want him to have easy access to a gun. I don't want him having access to a modem."

"How do I open this goddamn thing?" my father asked. "Ach! I give up."

"Dad, let me have it," I said, taking the bottle from him and opening it.

"Open it for me, that's all."

"This is where the 'thank you' goes."

"I said thank you."

"No, you didn't."

"I didn't?"

"No, you didn't."

I looked at Ivan as my father inadvertently squirted what seemed like half the bottle on his plate.

"A gun? You sure?"

On the way home that night, my father asked, "Where did you get all that from?"

"Oh, that stuff? I read. What can I tell you?"

"You're so stark, but you're right. I didn't pay in enough, and look at me."

"Right. Have you thanked me, the taxpayers, for taking care of you in your old age?"

"Why should I? I won the war."

A few months later, his blood pressure, which was always a little high, started spiking. He then started losing weight and his ankles started swelling. I made an appointment with his doctor, who happened to be a female Nigerian internist. What could go wrong there?

"Where is she from, Ba?" he asked after leaving the office.

"Nigeria."

"Nigeria?"

"Nigeria."

"Wow-we-wow! And she's in the medical field here in Las Vegas?"

"Medical field? Yes, the medical field. She's a doctor, Dad."

"I know, I know. What's her name, again?"

"Listen closely: Ezanalou. She's been your doctor for years."

"What's that name again? EZ Lou?"

"Close enough."

"What did she say about me?"

"You need to see a cardiologist."

"You mean for the heart?"

"Yes."

"What else did she say?"

"That was it."

"She didn't say anything to you while I wasn't listening?"

"No, I would tell you."

"No, you wouldn't."

"You don't trust?"

"No."

"Very nice."

My father's cardiologist, as it turned out, was a woman from Ukraine. The fun continued. At this first appointment, as she put the stethoscope to his chest, she asked him to be quiet.

"How does Moses make tea?" he asked.

"Shhh," she said in a Ukrainian accent.

"He . . . brews it."

Nothing.

"Shhh."

"What?"

"Shhh."

"Dad, don't talk."

"Don't talk?"

"Shhh."

"Dad, stop talking."

"Mr. Friedman, do you drink?" the doctor asked.

"What do you mean?"

"Do you drink?"

"Drink?"

"Dad, I think she means alcohol."

"Oh, yeah, yeah, big drinker."

"You are?" she asked.

"Well, not big, but, you know, I drink."

"Dad, you don't drink that much."

"You don't know."

"Doctor," I said, "he probably has about two to three drinks a week."

"Yeah, that's about right. I really don't drink that much."

EZ Lou once asked him if there was any violence in the household or if he was afraid of anyone.

"I don't think so," he replied. "No, not really." He looked at me. "I live alone."

It was revealed that he had atrial fibrillation, so they prescribed Coumadin, a drug he was on until he got to Tulsa. His doctor there, a dear friend, John Schumann, said the side effects weren't worth it.

"You know — what's your name again?" my father asked John, a doctor he had already been seeing for about a year.

"John Schumann."

"The pills are very good you put me on. And the way Barry lays them out in the tray, you know . . . the tray. Very easy. I take them, that's all."

The tray, mind you, was plastic and divided each day's pills into morning and evening. You didn't need to be a member of Mensa to fill them.

"See, John," I said, "forget your Yale degree, your residency, the fact you're president of the University of Oklahoma here in Tulsa — the key to medicine is putting the pills in the plastic trays."

"I agree."

After we left the clinic: "He's a nice guy."

"He really is. And a great doctor."

"You two know each other?"

"We're friends."

"So you know him?"

"Yeah."

"Did you know him before me?"

"Yes."

"Does he know I'm the father?"

I'm the father!

"I just take vitamins, right?"

"Dad, you're on, like, five blood-pressure medicines, a choles-
terol pill, and something for your indigestion.

"Wow-we-wow! Why?"

"You have high blood pressure."

"How bad is it?"

"Bad enough to be on five different pills."

"I didn't know."

"Of course you knew."

"I did?"

"You did."

"And the doctor prescribed these pills?"

"No, I decided. Of course the doctor prescribed them."

"Why couldn't someone just put heroin in a prescription
bottle and take it through security at the airport that way?
What, they're going to check? They're not going to check. And
if they do, you just tell them it's a prescription that comes in
powder form, that's all."

"I don't know why we're talking about heroin, but I don't
think that will work. They're going to check."

"They're not going to check."

"They have dogs that check for drugs."

"Dogs? Dogs. Ach, dogs. Dogs are going to know?"

"These dogs will know."

That my father could easily move from a discussion of his pills on a plastic tray to one about smuggling heroin through airport security, drug-sniffing dogs notwithstanding, is one of the reasons I wrote this book.

Nobody moves the conversation along any faster.

2012

∾

FOR THE FIRST eight years that my father was in Las Vegas, first in the apartment on South Pavilion Center Drive and then in the house he bought on Tumble Brook Drive in Sun City, I did not make a concerted effort to chronicle his life, generally, as he approached 90, nor my life with him, specifically, when I'd visit him or he'd visit me or we'd talk on the phone. I'd occasionally post a story on Facebook, but that was about it. I soon noticed, though, there was an interest, bordering on fascination, about his life and, if I may be so immodest, our relationship. I was both flattered and bemused. "Sons who write about their fathers" is pretty standard literary fare, but there was something about stories about Jack Friedman that my Facebook followers — and I had about 1,000 at the time — looked forward to.

At one point, I can't remember when exactly, I told him I was writing about him and posting the stories on Facebook.

"What do you mean, 'posting'?"

"Oh, boy. It's like a journal entry and people get to comment."

"What do you mean?"

"They comment on what I write."

"Where?"

"On the computer."

"What? They write on the screen?"

"Sort of, yeah. Anyway, you OK with this? Me writing about you?"

"What are you writing about me? What do I say?"

"This — just who you are, what you do, your outlook on life. You're funny, alive. People seem interested."

"Are you getting rich off my fame?"

"Dad, you have no idea how many parts of that last question are incorrect and hilarious."

WHAT FOLLOWS IN THIS CHAPTER, and the chapters that follow, are those entries. They came in spurts, usually when I'd go to visit him for a week or two, whether I was working at Sin City or another comedy club in Vegas or not, or when he came to visit me in Tulsa, where I was living. Additionally, many of the conversations, as you'll see, are just phone calls. I can see now, as I review these posts — and, again, that's what they were originally — how his level of engagement and cognition through the years deteriorated, even though, as my sister/his daughter, Susan (and I often had to remind him they were one and the same), mentioned to me once that our father, as sweet and as good-natured as he is and was, was never as interested in what people were saying to him as much as he was in what he was saying in response. His asking a question, the literal sound of his voice, was the point of the conversation for him — not the answer from the person to whom he was talking, in this case me. So, for instance, if he would ask me how many books I had written and what they were about, he was already losing interest in the topic as soon as the words left his lips.

I say this more charitably than it sounds, but my father couldn't hear, didn't listen, had no short-term memory, and didn't care.

It was the perfect storm. It was Jack Friedman.

WHAT FOLLOWS IN VOLUME ONE, as mentioned, are actual status updates on Facebook in the years 2012-2016.

The first entry I found on Facebook was about a month before the 2012 election, when my father and I were visiting his brother and sister-in-law, Leo and Marilyn, my aunt and uncle.

16 OCTOBER

Delray Beach, Florida

Aunt Marilyn, 89, was yelling at the television and at Romney, who during his debate with Obama talked of investment income, the earning power of real Americans, and how he, Romney, hoped to lessen their tax liability.

"We don't have investment income!" Marilyn screamed.

"Who are you screaming at?" Leo asked, finishing the fruit slices and pretzel M&Ms that Marilyn had laid out for snacks during the debate. "Anyway, I think Obama got him."

"If Obama wins next month," I added, "remember this night. It may be why."

"One of the guys I run with in Vegas said there's no way this country was going to elect a schvartze," my father added.

"Dad, does he know Obama is already president?"

"The guy's an idiot," he said of the guy in Vegas. "He says he still can't believe the country did that and swears they won't do it again. I tell him, 'What? Mr. Bush was better?' "

Somewhat endearing, I thought — odd, but endearing — the honorific before Bush's name.

When we left tonight and because we were leaving to fly back home — my dad to Vegas and me to Tulsa — Marilyn gave me another bag of fruit slices, unopened, and three cans of Coke for my flight back.

Driving to the Best Western Plus in Boca Raton, after leaving

Marilyn and Leo's, even though there were no Obama-Biden yard signs, nothing on Military Highway to let you think there was anyone even running against Romney-Ryan, and even though we still passed the billboard of Obama bowing to a sheik on I-95, I couldn't help thinking the conversation had changed because of the debate. The anxiety was back to manageable levels, the president was good.

My president was good.

The night was good. I broke into the fruit slices before we got back to the hotel.

I looked over and my father was asleep.

THIS WAS the only entry noting a date in 2012. I'm sure in the compiling of the next few years, some of the memories from that year will pop up.

2

2013

2 February

2 "Who can do this kind of eating all the time?" my father asks, as we head to the Red Rock Casino for the $6.95 all-you-can-eat breakfast buffet.

"But you love the buffets. Enjoy yourself."

"What do you mean, 'Enjoy myself'? I don't want to get fat."

"What do you care if you get fat? You're 86."

"What if I find myself in a strange bedroom?"

"No one will be more surprised than the woman whose bedroom you're in."

"Yeah, but you can't eat like this all the time. You'd be, like, 400 pounds."

"Then let's stop coming to them."

"But I got the coupons, so what am I going to do? Not use them?"

"That's exactly what many people conclude, yes."

A FEW WEEKS BACK, last time I was here, I noticed his refrigerator wouldn't stay shut on the same day I noticed the toilet in the guest bedroom wouldn't stop running. As I was headed back to Oklahoma that morning, I asked if he knew a plumber he could call, as I couldn't get one to the house before I left.

"Yeah, yeah, I got a plumber who's a friend."

"Since when do you have a plumber for a friend?"

"Don't worry about it. You don't know him."

"I'm not worried about it. I didn't expect you to have a friend who's a plumber. I'm just surprised by that."

"I do his taxes. I don't charge him."

I arrived here last night, and the refrigerator door would still not close and the toilet was still running.

"Dad, I thought you were going to get the fridge and toilet fixed."

"I did."

"No, you didn't. They're still broken."

"I called him, I'm telling you. He came by."

"What did he do?"

"What did he do? I don't know what he did. He fixed it."

"Well, he did a lousy job because they're both still broken."

"But he didn't charge me anything."

23 FEBRUARY

Remember yesterday's total ban on buffets? Well, it's been lifted. We're at the Suncoast Hotel St. Tropez buffet now because, yes, he's got a coupon and what are we supposed to do? Not use it?

"Hey, Dad, I thought we weren't doing buffets anymore?"

"Yeah, I know, but they have the variety."

Like a plumber who isn't very good, bad food is excusable if there's a lot of it. But there is now a problem.

As I stood waiting for my father to present the coupons to the cashier, I could tell he was aggravated by something.

"The miserable bastards," he said as he returned to me,

folding the receipt.

"What happened?"

"They wouldn't comp the buffet."

"Why not?"

"I don't know. They said that the coupon expired."

"Did it?"

"I don't know. We're done with this place after today. Let's go in. We're going to kill them. We're going to eat the world."

24 February

Noticed on the way to the Suncoast this afternoon, before heading to the airport, my father's car is once again making a grinding sound.

"Dad, the brakes are going out again. I don't know how that's possible, but they are."

"I don't hear anything."

"That's because you're deaf."

"What?"

"Perfect."

"You can't hear."

"I can hear fine. You mumble."

"I don't mumble. And you don't hear that squeaking."

"Squeaking? What kind of squeaking?"

"Squeaking-squeaking. How many different kinds of squeaking are there?"

"It's fine."

∿

25 February

He calls.

"You know, you're right. There's something wrong with the car."

"You mean the squeak."

"It's more of a grind."

"Fine, it's a grind."

"Well, you said it was a squeak the other day, and I just wanted you to know it's more of a rubbing, you know — it's a grind."

"All right! It's a grind."

"I just wanted you to know I heard it."

"OK."

"Otherwise, nothing special, everything is fine. Just wanted you to know it wasn't a squeak."

"But you'll take care of it."

"Yeah, but it's a grind — not a squeak."

"ALL RIGHT!"

2 APRIL

My daughter, Nina, and I just arrived in Vegas nine minutes ago. After our brief stay, we're headed up to Medford, Oregon, where she is moving in with her boyfriend, from France, a wine-maker — very romantic stuff. She and Aureliene will probably get married soon. A little off topic, but I remember at one point Auri was worried about whether or not he could stay, whether immigration would throw him out. Melissa, my girlfriend, said, "Auri, really, don't worry. Customs has a lot more people they're going to throw out of the country before they get to cute French winemakers."

Anyway, about my stay here with Nina: She wanted to come see her grandfather because she, too, wondered how many more times she'd get to see him, plus she hadn't been to Vegas in years. She and her brother used to come when I was performing regularly at the Maxim and the MGM Grand. I used to get them virgin daiquiris and they'd hang out in our room while I was onstage. She's 25 now so will probably demand some rum in that daiquiri if she orders one. The biggest problem, as I see it, is that we're here for two and a half days and my father has already notified us he has coupons for each one of those meals, which, of course, will all be at buffets. We need to go eat in the next few minutes because a quick math check says there's no way to make these numbers work otherwise.

3 APRIL

At the Suncoast, I notice there's a Neil Diamond impersonator and something called the Jewish Repertory Theatre of Nevada doing the play Love Letters.

"Hey, Nina, I wonder what that's like: first letter from the Jewish husband to his wife, 'Go to hell,' and then she writes back, 'Kiss my ass!' "

Judging from her reaction, she doesn't find that as funny as I do.

4 APRIL

Nina is struggling.

"Dad, I just can't do this anymore. How many more buffets do we have left?"

"This one," I tell her, "and then the one tonight."

"I'm not going to make it."

"Yeah, you will. I have faith in you."

After the breakfast buffet, we took my father back to the house and went to New York-New York Casino to ride the roller coaster.

"Dad, you won't lose any 'Dad' points if you don't go on the roller coaster with me, but you'd score many, many points if you did."

Of course I went after that.

On the way back to Summerlin and my father's, Nina was dreading dinner.

"I just can't do another buffet. I'm serious. I've never been more sick in my life."

"Amateur."

And just as I did for her, she did for me. She went to the buffet with us. She had salad only, but she went.

The Friedmans know about love.

6 MAY

Once again, we're headed to Boca Raton, Delray, and Boynton Beach to see Leo and Marilyn; my father's friends Jerry and Marvin; and Ida, Jerry Parker, and one of the Selmas (I'm not sure if this is the Pitsy or not). Marilyn asked tonight if Ben's Delicatessen is OK for dinner (when isn't it?). Thirteen Jews at dinner all asking for separate checks. It's why waitresses and waiters in South Florida have PTSD.

7 MAY

Military Trail, the 46.2-mile six-lane north-south arterial road in Broward and Palm Beach counties in South Florida, is Purgatory. Every time I look up it seems I'm on this fucking road. Dinner tonight, at some Italian place (not Macaroni Grill), wasn't bad, except the bread came not with butter but hummus, which is expressly forbidden in the ancient Jewish texts. On the way — I was driving — I couldn't find the place.

"Take Military Trail," Leo said.

"Of course that's what I should take."

At dinner, my father approached the hummus as he would an alien from Planet *Zargon*.

"What is this fakakta butter?"

"It's not butter, Dad. It's called hummus."

"Savages!" he said, sticking his fork in a glob of it and putting it on his bread.

9 MAY

Today, Leo, Marilyn, my father, and I decided to take a drive to the beach. As we were driving through a town called Leisure-ville, we passed a place of business with a sign that read "Media-tion Center."

"Look, Marilyn," I said, "a Mediation Center."

"What?"

"It's a Mediation Center."

"Medication Center?" asked my father. "Like a hospital?"

"What kind of Dedication Center is it?" asked Leo.

"No, no—"

"What? Dedication—" said my father.

"Media—" I started to say.

"Jack, it's not medical," Marilyn said, trying to help clarify things.

"What?" Leo asked.

This went on for about 10 minutes, each one incorrectly correcting the others' in-corrections.

We find the beach, we find parking. The beach, however, is over a small incline, so we can't really see the water. What we can see are people walking to the beach. Do we get out of the car?

You have to ask?

We simply rolled down the windows.

Leo pointed.

"It's over there," he said.

"Where?" my father asked, sitting up.

"There." Leo pointed again.

"Must be nice," I said.

"It's a beach. Oh, yeah, yeah, I see the sand," my father said.

That certainly settled it.

We see people in bathing suits walking toward the beach we will not get out of the car to see.

Five minutes tops we're there.

"OK, ready to go?" asked Leo.

On the way back to Delray, we start planning dinner.

Later that evening, at dinner, Leo told the story of attending a birthday party for a woman who had just turned 100.

"I dance with her for about 20 seconds. Have a nice life, whatever, go in peace. Now, another guy takes my place. 'She's all yours,' I'm thinking. The story is this: I notice he's dancing and dancing and dancing with her and he's twirling her around and he's bending her and then twirling her again. This must go on for how long I don't know, and I'm thinking to myself, 'Jesus Christ, what are you doing? You're going to kill this old broad.' "

∽

10 MAY

My father and I arrive at Marilyn and Leo's around noon.

"Why is it so goddamn cold here?" my father asks, not even in the front door.

"Because, Jack!" says Marilyn.

We come into the living room, just as Leo is getting up from the chair in which he always sits.

"Leo, where you going?" my father asks.

He doesn't answer.

"Where'd he go?" my father asks Marilyn, who is now in the living room.

"Went to get the mail."

"What kind of hail?"

"The mail!"

"Oh, I thought you said 'hail.' "

"Mail!"

I know very little in life, but I do know to never interrupt an old Jewish man on his way to get mail. Especially if that old Jewish man is a former postman, which Leo is.

At dinner — we're at TooJay's, a place like Ben's, only TooJay's isn't kosher (or maybe it's the other way around) — and Leo, I can tell, is not happy. For starters, Marilyn forgot the coupon that would have enabled us to receive half off one entree with every full-price meal.

It's not the price, it's the principle, apparently.

"You had one thing to remember," Leo says to his wife.

"Why didn't you remember?" Marilyn asks.

"Was I supposed to remember?"

"I forgot, Leo, OK? Shoot me!"

I think: Sixty-eight years of marriage — how many times have they had this conversation?

Dinner was at 6:30, which is later than either Marilyn or Leo wanted to eat, but Ida wanted to meet at Selma's at 4:00 to get together with the family and, as Ida put it, "to have a nosh first."

"So we're going to eat for two and a half hours," Leo asks, "before we eat?"

"Maybe she won't have anything to eat," says Marilyn.

"She'll have, she'll have."

And then Leo starts singing to himself, as he does most days — ba-da-dee, bad-da-dum. It is not a happy tune this time.

11 MAY

Wyndham Hotel, Boca Raton, Friday night

I'm probably not going to do this story justice. . . .

Today at lunch, we met my father's cousin Judy and her husband, Gary, who are both in their seventies and both retired, for lunch. He was wearing blue shorts and support hose and a big black brace from his ankles to his knees to ward off edema; she was in an ankle cast from a fall, and a wrist brace from trying to break that fall. Black-and-blue marks, discolorations, other mixed-color bruises ran up and down both of her arms. Life, for her the past few months, she tells us, has not been easy even before the fall, as she has had to undergo extensive blood work. It's taken its toll. She looks tired, tentative. As the lunch progressed, pictures start getting passed around: my father, my mother; Leo, Marilyn; and then Gary and Judy. First photos of their grandson's wedding, then their granddaughters in matching blue dresses, and then Gary shows me his and Judy's wedding photo. They're in the hallway of a synagogue. He, fit and trim, in a tailored suit and wearing Buddy Holly glasses; Judy in a dress, the tiniest of waists, smiling at her new husband.

"Thirty-five years ago," he says to me, pointing at the photo on his iPhone. "Look, wasn't she a beautiful woman." And then this man in the support hose with the edema looks at his wife with the bruises and the cast and the brace who is, at the moment, eating French toast, smiles, and says, "Ah, but look, she still is."

Later that evening.

There was a large family gathering tonight, including Ida and her new "fella" at some restaurant that serves both soup and salad, not just one with the entree. Plus, Ida had a coupon. There was some discussion tonight about whether the restaurant should have added the 15 percent gratuity, because while it was true we were a party of eight, it was also true we got separate checks. Ida, who knows this place well enough to know that the $42.81 she was billed for her and her "fella's" meal was not right. She called over the non-English-speaking Russian waitress and bitched. Best line at dinner goes to Selma — I still don't know if this one is the Pitsy — who is still not over the illegality of the previous administration.

"How is it possible that Cheney isn't rotting in some jail somewhere?"

On the way back to Marilyn and Leo's, we discussed the finer points of weather.

"Is this rain, or what?" my father asked, as water hit the windshield.

"Of course it's rain, Jack!" said Marilyn.

"Maybe it's dew," said my father.

"It's drizzling," said Leo.

"It's rain," Marilyn insisted.

∿

12 MAY

We went to see my father's old friend Jerry today. Back in New York in the 60s, Jerry was in the pornographic-novelty business and my father was his accountant. Jerry still has small artifacts from those days, including — and he gave each of us one — a plastic male-and-female key chain that you can join at the groin. He must have done all right because his house is enormous. It's got a pool, and his wife — I think it's his fourth — adores him. Jerry, too, has had some medical problems lately, including a skin graft on his elbow, which he keeps pinching.

"The doctor told me to stop doing this, as I was making it worse, but I don't know what the hell to do."

"Maybe stop pinching it?" I ask.

"Yeah, I should," he says, putting both arms down. "Plus, now there's something with my heart. I don't know. This sucks."

Just then his dog jumped up on his lap.

"This is my little fella. I got him classified as an emotional-support animal. I don't really need it," he adds, "but I love my fella. I won't travel without him, not that I'm going anywhere."

13 MAY

My father has begun counting fountains.

"One, two, three," he'll say, looking out the window as we drive by them. "How many fountains they got in this state?"

"How many?"

"Yeah, how many?"

"I have no idea."

"My question's academic."

14 MAY

We're at Flakowitz of Boynton, a deli, having breakfast. It is 9:15 a.m., meaning it's 6:15 a.m. in Las Vegas.

"I'm going to call Jeannette," he says.

"Dad, it's 6:15 there."

"No, it's 12:15."

"Trust me, three hours earlier."

"I'm going to call. What the hell? She'll be up."

She wasn't up.

"What's the matter, you sound sick," I hear him say.

"It's Jack. . . . I can't understand you. What are you talking about, butter and what side of the bread it's buttered on? What the hell are you talking about? I know, I know, I forgot to call. We've been busy."

He hangs up.

"What does she want from my life?"

∿

15 MAY

Back at Flakowitz, in large part because it offers free pastry before the meal and then, say, if you order a bagel, you get cream cheese and butter for the same price. For breakfast, we usually alternate between here and the all-you-can-eat buffet at Seminole Casino Coconut Creek, which is $4.95 and includes beverages and the omelet station. We'd go there every day, but as we know, you can't eat like that all the time. You'd be 400 pounds. Can't beat the variety, though.

∿

26 MAY

Back home in Tulsa.

Aunt Marilyn called to tell me she thinks Norris Cole will be the key to the Miami Heat's playoff success or failure.

∿

1 JUNE

Sad news.

Marvin Kraftchin, the one and only Marvin Kraftchin in all of America, died. His daughter, Rhonda, called my father and said that the day he died, she went to his condo and found my father's message on his answering machine. We had tried reaching him last month.

"Of the 15 guys I grew up with, Barry," my dad said on the phone a few minutes ago, using my full name for a change, "there's only three left: me, Jerry Parker, who married Pitsy, and Mel, who lives in Fullerton, California, I think. All right, listen, Marvin, he did all right. He wasn't cut short."

"Maybe you should call Mel, huh?"

"Yeah, maybe so. The last time I called, though, his girlfriend — he's not married — picked up and said he was napping. He takes a lot of naps."

"You called once and he was napping. It doesn't mean he's always napping. Call him, Dad. He's an old friend."

"Maybe later. I hear he naps."

16 JUNE

It's 12:30 a.m. and my father, who is in Tulsa for a visit and just got here today, wants to go to Walmart. Why? He needs tan pants. Could this purchase not wait until morning?

Perhaps.

"How are you, sir?" the cashier asks.

"Got a half hour, I'll tell you the whole story — or wait for the movie. It's in color."

This is beyond wonderful to me. My father still thinks clarifying that the movie is in color is the selling point people need to see the movie of his life.

17 JUNE

We're at breakfast at Village Inn. He likes the coffee here, even though, considering the amount of artificial sweetener and Half & Half he puts in it, I can't imagine it makes much of a difference. Anyway, my father is burning through material.

"You're a gentleman," my father says to the waiter. "I saw you coming out of a room that said so."

Meanwhile the busboy has forgotten my father's half-and-half.

"You'll hear from my lawyer," my father says to him, "as soon as he gets out of jail."

The waitress brings him an extra plate of white toast because she thought the first plate she brought him was undercooked.

"Sir, I thought I'd bring you another plate of toast."

"If you did windows, I'd marry you," he tells her.

"I'm already married."

"Does your husband know?"

"I hope so."

"May you never know the horror of stretch marks."

AT LUNCH I took him to Mario's Pizzeria.

"There must be a Mario's in every city in the country. Why all the Marios?"

"Why all the Marios? I don't know how to answer that."

"Are they really all from New York?"

"I doubt it."

"No, because you always see the name Mario. I assume they're from New York."

"There are Marios all over the country."

"Mario, nu? Don't misunderstand me. He makes a good pie."

The waitress came by.

"How was your spaghetti Bolognese, sir?" she asks my father.

"Better than sex."

Later that night, back at the house, we were watching *Lonesome Dove*, and my father was not impressed.

"This is the dumbest Western I've ever seen. I don't even know who's who."

18 JUNE

We were at breakfast this morning — we usually go out — and the waiter came by with a pot of decaf.

"Would you like some more?" he asked my father.

"Is Bismarck a herring?"

The waiter looked confused.

"Yeah, he wants some more," I said.

My father usually holds off on the Bismarck line, going instead with the "Is the Pope Catholic?" or "Is 58 the atomic weight of cobalt?" when asked a question that requires an immediate, unambiguous "yes." If you're wondering how it is my father knows the atomic weight of cobalt, you haven't been following closely enough. The Bismarck story is more interesting. There was a guy named Johann Wiechmann, who had a store in Stralsund, Germany, in the late 1800s that sold fish. His wife, Karoline, prepared the herring. Wiechmann evidently admired Otto von Bismarck and sent the then-chancellor of Germany a barrel of his wife's herring on Bismarck's birthday. Wiechmann kept sending these packages of herring for years, and finally he asked Bismarck if he could call his herring Bismarck Herring? Bismarck agreed. Bismarck Herring, then, is a type of herring, not a company name. It is trimmed into a single filet and cut into shorter lengths, unlike rollmops, which are double pieces of herring, rolled together, and usually kept paired with a toothpick. Why my father would think anyone would know that, or about Wiechmann and his wife and the chancellor — much less why a waiter with a pot of decaf in Tulsa, Oklahoma, would — is beyond my comprehension.

But it is one of the oddities and wonders of Jack Friedman.

TODAY, we also drove by a fruit stand. Before the fruit stand, which has a sign that reads "Fruit," is a sign that reads "Fruit Up Ahead." In front of the fruit stand, again where there is a sign that says "Fruit," are crates of apples, bananas, peaches, plums, and grapes.

"What do they sell here, Barry?" my father asks as we get out of the car. "Fruit?"

"Yeah."

"Fruit, you mean?"

"I mean fruit. Would you like some fruit, Dad?"

"Nah. Fruit? I don't know. Fruit. Yeah, I don't know. Maybe."

AT NIGHT we went to dinner at Jason's Deli.

"What do you mean, no coffee?" my father asks toward the end of the meal, when he couldn't find a pot of coffee at the self-serve.

"I think they have coffee, Dad, I just don't think they have any left."

"What kind of state is this?"

"I don't know if it's Oklahoma's fault."

"They're savages! This is a restaurant, right?"

"Yes."

"What's the matter with these people?"

"I don't think you should be taking this personally."

"How do you not serve coffee?"

"They serve coffee — just not at this particular moment."

"Oklahoma! Nu, Oklahoma?"

19 JUNE

This morning, at breakfast at Old School Bagel Cafe, which he has inexplicably been calling Owl Head Bagels, he was admiring Melissa's new haircut — she has cut it very short. My father has a magic with women that is indescribable.

"I like your hair," he said to her. "You look like a young boy. Really, it takes 10 years off you."

"You really want to talk about hair, Jack?" Melissa asked, pointing to his toupee.

Tonight, we watched a basketball game on television. NBA analyst Jack Friedman remarked, "It's becoming a body sport, you know?"

20 JUNE

This morning — my father has been staying with us, so we gave him our bed and moved upstairs — I saw him with a copy of *TulsaPeople*, a magazine for which I write a monthly column, when I came downstairs in the morning. He wasn't reading it, he was using it as a placemat while doing his crossword puzzle.

"Dad, you know I'm in that."

"What do you mean?"

"In the magazine. I write for them."

"I know, I know."

"Did you read it?"

"What do you mean?"

"Did you read it."

"Where?"

"Look."

I opened the magazine and showed him. "Here."

He turned the page.

"You're not going to read it."

"I don't know what the hell you're talking about."

"Astonishing."

"No, I saw it, I saw it. Very nice. They pay you?"

"Yeah, a little."

My brother, Wayne, happened to call. He's in California.

"The place used to be glamorous," my father said of the state after he hung up, "but it's tarnished now, rusty. Forty percent of the people are starving to death and the other half can't speak English. You couldn't pay me to move there. Don't misunderstand me, I'm sure there are some nice places there."

The "don't misunderstand me" makes it art, I think.

We then went out for a drive and went past the praying hands at Oral Roberts University.

"Give me money!" my father yelled. "Give me money!" He held out his cupped hands.

"You remember coming here with Mom?"

"Yeah, yeah, yeah."

"No, you don't."

"I kind of remember. I'm telling you, Ba, after your mother and I got back together, it was the best part of the whole goddamn marriage."

21 JUNE

"In Oklahoma, you grow hay, wheat, and oats, right?" he asked this morning on the way to breakfast.

"We grow hay? Yes, we do. I mean, I don't know. Can you even grow hay?"

"In Nevada, I don't think there's a farm in the whole state. It's too arid. Italy is the same way."

"I'm sure there are farms in both places."

"Well, you know what I mean. . . . So is it hot outside or is it cold? Because outside, I'm hot. Inside, like now, I'm cold."

"That's because it's, like, a million degrees out there and we have the air conditioner on in here."

"Yeah, that's probably it."

All this before breakfast. We finally arrived at the Village Inn. The waitress came over.

"I want two eggs, sunny side," my father said, "but don't turn them. I want the eggs lying intimately over well-done white toast."

22 JUNE

Tough to know what story to end with, as my father's going home today, but 34 years ago, my mom, after deciding to reunite with my father — they had been apart 18 months — had driven 1,400 miles from Broken Arrow, Oklahoma, to Greenlawn, New York, and was sitting in the living room of the house that she had stormed out of a year and a half earlier, talking with my dad.

It was late.

"Jack, I'm exhausted. I think I need to go to bed."

"Of course," he said. "We'll talk more tomorrow."

"Well, it's been almost two years, Jack. I don't know where to go. Where do I sleep?"

"You sleep with the owner."

I don't know why I was thinking about that, but whenever I see him, whenever one of us leaves the other, I think about it being the last time I will see him. He's 86 He's in great shape. But he's 86.

He then called while he was on the plane, before it had taken off.

"I just ate half the turkey sandwich you made me," he said. "My God, it was the best sandwich I had ever eaten. The turkey, the mustard, the bread . . . delicious!"

23 JUNE

He called today at 8 a.m. (6 a.m. PST).

"I want you to know, Ba, you changed my life. I went out and bought turkey and bread when I got home. I realized I had no mustard, so I went back. I have never had mustard on a turkey sandwich before. What a combination!"

"I think we've been through this, but what do you usually put on your turkey sandwiches?"

"Ketchup."

"So you like it with mustard, huh?"

"Unbelievable! Who knew to put mustard on turkey?"

"Other than the world's 7.1 billion people, probably nobody."

"I guess so. But thanks again. I'm going to make one now. You put the mustard on both sides, right?"

"It's six in the morning where you are. You want turkey now?"

"Yeah, what the hell! All right, love you, sweetheart. Best to Melissa."

∽

12 AUGUST

My father called tonight to tell me his oven door broke, but because he doesn't cook much, he added, he decided that instead of buying a new unit he'd just use some masking tape to keep "the door up there so it doesn't flop down."

"The oven still works, Ba, it still works. I use it to make a steak once in a while."

"You put a steak in the oven?"

"I mean, sometimes I cook it on top, sometimes on the bottom. I mostly only use the burners."

Just then he got another call.

"Hold on."

Back then, my father could maneuver the call-waiting feature almost flawlessly.

He returned.

"That was Bill. He wanted to borrow a propane torch."

"What would make him think you have a propane torch, (A), and (B), if you have one, why do you have one?"

"I got, I got."

"No, you don't."

"I don't have."

"No."

"What happened to it?"

"You never had a propane torch."

"I thought I did. You know, Bill's a retired cop from Gary, Indiana."

24 AUGUST

In which my father calls and puts dentistry and his pending death in much-needed perspective.

He calls.

"Ba, I'm not having any more work done on my teeth."

"Why not?"

"Ah, this stupid dentist — he said I needed three crowns and a bridge."

"Maybe he's right.

"I'm not suggesting he's wrong, but 3,000 bucks! That's way out of whack."

"But you have the money."

"That's not the point. I could be dead in two years. Then what do I do with them? It's not worth it."

25 AUGUST

In which my father calls and puts someone else's death in much-needed perspective.

"Ba, did you know Sus?"

"Sus? No."

"You know Sus!"

"I don't know Sus."

"I thought you knew Sus."

"I don't know Sus. Who's Sus?"

"Sus!"

"You can keep saying it, I'm still not going to know who he is."

"Sus! Anyway, he was one of the guys. He died. He was in the group. There were three Jews — me, him, and another guy. He was one of them. Anyway, pancreatic cancer got him. 83. A quiet guy, good bowler!"

"I'm sorry, Dad."

"Anyway, I'm playing pinochle tonight."

31 AUGUST

Looking on Facebook tonight, looking over the posts about my father, I noticed he has a Facebook account. Why? God himself is no doubt perplexed by that. My father, according to the page, has 11 friends, "likes" the movie Super 8, and the last activity I see is when a woman named Dawn wished him a happy birthday in 2012. Previous activity: when the woman named Dawn wished him a happy birthday in 2011.

I sent him a Friend request.

And now I wait.

SEPTEMBER

❧

1 September

My dad calls. It's noisy.

"So, Ba, I took your advice."

"I didn't give any. What did I do?"

"I am at the Suncoast and I just won $119 playing Crap, but that's not important. They're comping me dinner at the buffet. I'm going to destroy them, Ba, destroy them!"

"Yes indeed, because nothing bankrupts the Boyd Gaming Corporation faster than an 86-year-old man going back for a second piece of pie. That's great, Dad, but what advice did I give you that you're thanking me for?"

"You told me to move here . . . to Vegas."

3 September
He calls.
"Barry, I bowled terribly today. TERRIBLY! But I had great control and felt strong."

12 September
It was open phone lines with Jack Friedman today, as he called a lot. Probably best if I just highlight the proceedings.

9 a.m.: "Hey, Ba, a question: I have a doctor thing coming up, a dentist. How much cheaper will it be if I just died?"

"Much cheaper, actually. How you feeling?"

"Nah, it's not that. Jesus Christ, is this costing me! By the way, I love you, I swear to God!"

11 a.m.: "These fucking nurses. They call, give me six numbers. 8-7-4-5-7-6. Talk a little slower when you're leaving a message, for crying out loud."

"What were they calling about?"

"I don't know. They wanted me to call them back."

"But you couldn't."

"No, I did. I got the number, it's not that. But talk slower."

3 p.m.: "Nevada doesn't have a state income tax. No wonder they're so stupid."

"But doing tax returns is easier, right?"

"Good point."

5:30 p.m.: "My friends, always with Obama: 'He spends too much, he spends too much.' 'Yeah?' I tell them. 'How about Mr.

Bush and his weapons of mass destruction?' He spends 16 trillion dollars and finds bupkis."

"Did they understand 'bupkis'?"

"The Jews do."

6 p.m.: "I'm going to dinner tonight. Everyone in the group gets to choose. Today someone chose Mexican. What kind of fakakta Mexican? What kind of people are they, these Mexicans? It's the worst food. What is it, the sauce? Is it the sauce that makes it Mexican?"

"Order something that's not Mexican."

"I'm going to order something that's not Mexican."

"Good idea."

13 September

It's Yom Kippur today, the holiest day for Jews, a day in which we are supposed to fast to concentrate on our wrongdoings over the previous year. Jews are not supposed to put themselves in danger from fasting, so if they have a medical condition, they are allowed to eat. This reminds me that a few years back, my father and I went to a synagogue after he first moved out to Las Vegas.

"Dad, you going to fast today?"

"No, I know myself. I'm going to get a headache."

He had a bowl of cereal.

We didn't know of a rabbi, didn't know of a congregation, but my rabbi here in Tulsa made a few calls and got us into a place — the "made a few calls" is such a Vegas thing to say, by the way. We got there early, before services started, and one of the ushers told us the service would start at 9:30 and about the Starbucks down the street where we could go before the service started. The synagogue was officiated by a husband-and-wife rabbi from Russia. There is a point in the Yom Kippur, a prayer, where congregants are asked to atone for their vanity, cruelty, disloyalty, judgmental behavior, anger, gossip, and shortsightedness . . . to name just a few of our transgressions against God. It's responsive reading where we, in the sanctuary, echo the rabbi, so he says, "Forgive us for being stiff-necked," and we repeat, "Forgive us for being stiff-necked." To the untrained ear, like my father's, this litany is insufferable.

"Jesus Christ," my father asked after hearing about all his shortcomings, "how fucking bad are we?"

We sat behind two women who had to be from New Jersey or New York. I could hear them whispering to each other — it was like they were on a subway. When it was time for responsive reading, they joined in, as did most of the congregation. In one of the greatest New York accents I ever heard, one of them said, "Oh, Lawd, we yearn fa ya love."

As we were leaving, I noticed there were tables with fruits and snacks lined up outside the sanctuary. This fast that Jews are supposed to do — it's supposed to go from sunup to sundown.

It was 1:30 p.m.

This is my kind of reformed Judaism.

21 September

I called to tell my father when my flight was arriving. He was on his way, he told me, to the Jewish War Veterans of Las Vegas buffet luncheon, but he wanted to write it down first.

"I'm coming in on American Flight 1022, Wednesday at two."

"That's American Flight 1022, Wednesday at two?"

"Yes."

"You know I'm going to the buffet. They're buying me lunch."

"I know. The flight, Dad, yes, you got it?"

"What is it again?"

"That's American Airlines, right? Flight 1022 on—"

"—Wednesday."

"Wednesday."

"At two."

"Afternoon or morning?"

"Afternoon, Dad."

"At the airport?"

"At the airport."

"Let me read it back to you."

He does.

"You know I got this buffet today?"

"I do. I'll see you in a few days."

"Let me know your flight information when you get a chance."

"Ah — OK, sure."

22 September

Will be flying to Vegas in a few days, but my father's friend Bill called this morning to tell me my dad had three glasses of wine last night at a party, seemed ready to pass out, complained of dizziness, so Bill called an ambulance.

I called my father's cell. He picked up. He was in the hospital.

"You OK? What happened? Bill told me you had three glasses of wine and passed out."

"What kind of three glasses? I had half a cup."

I talked to a nurse who said there was no heart attack, no stroke, but the hospital decided to keep him overnight.

I called back.

"You're going to be all right. They're going to keep you one more day."

"I swear to God, Ba, I'm walking out of here if they don't let me go. I'm going crazy. I feel fine, they're treating me good. I mean, I just want to go home. I don't want them to think I didn't like the service."

"The service? You don't want hospital personnel to think you didn't like their service? Who thinks like this?"

"You know, they've been fine. No problems. I just want to go home."

"I'll see you in a few days. Don't drink so much."

"I don't drink at all. I had a cup, maybe two."

"I heard. I'll be there soon."

"Don't worry. Everything is fine here. They're treating me well."

All joking aside, which is difficult with my father, as I hung up the phone, it occurred to me that he is getting to a point where he should not be living thousands of miles away from any of his children — just for moments like this.

25 September

I arrive. He's home from the hospital. We have plans tonight.

There is a seminar, "Essential Financial Strategies for the New Economy," to which he has been invited. The invitation that came in the mail was for dinner for two at Fleming's Steak House, if we listened to their pitch on such strategies.

It came to Jack Friedman, CPA.

"You come with me," he said on the phone earlier in the week. "I'll tell them you're my client."

"You want me to fly out to Vegas to get a free dinner?"

"They're buying. What the hell?"

"I'm coming anyway, but OK."

"Pretend you're a client," my father tells me again, now that I'm here, "or better yet, a CPA."

"Good idea, Dad. Two Friedmans, father and son, both lying about their credentials."

"It goes fast, Ba," he says before we leave the house. "I have been to these things before, but sometimes dinner doesn't start right away, so you better eat something beforehand, just in case. You want a hard-boiled egg?"

"Why would I want a hard-boiled egg?"

"I thought you might want one, that's all."

"I don't want a hard-boiled egg."

"You better eat something."

"Does it have to be a hard-boiled egg?"

"You don't like hard-boiled eggs?"

"It's not that I don't like them — it's just . . . OK, give me an egg."

We arrive at Fleming's. My father is holding the invitation.

"A guy named Bradley Zucker . . . gotta be Jewish," says my father, reading the card as we walk in. "Look at all the wine on the shelf. Grab one."

"You want me to steal a bottle of wine?"

"No, they let you have them."

"No, they don't."

The program starts. Zucker starts screaming almost immediately.

"Is money falling through the cracks of your fingers?" he asks. "Well, is it?"

"Let me check," my dad answers loud enough for people around him to hear. He then tells the guy sitting next to him that he is a graduate from Columbia University in New York City, which isn't exactly accurate. My father took a semester of accounting at North Georgia College before being shipped overseas, but a lot of people confuse the two universities.

"There's a bottle of wine behind you. Grab it," he says to me.

"Again? I'm not stealing bottles of wine."

"Ach!"

"Be proactive," Zucker says. "There's a fictional widow named Annie, who did not do the proper proactive planning. I could have helped her. And there's a fictional husband, Alan, who did not do right by his fictional wife, Lydia, with that real-estate investment. I am trained in science, economics, and mathematics. Who told you not to buy Facebook?" He answers his own question. "I did. Remember, the game is won in the second half."

"Who's Alan?" my father asks me. "And is he with Annie or Lydia?"

"I don't know," I whisper.

"He's definitely Jewish," my father says.

I don't ask if he was talking about Alan or Zucker.

Dinner, as mentioned, is included — and the salmon was not bad, actually — along with one beverage, which as it turns blew up the whole evening. My father orders a root beer with his steak (always a good combination), but when dessert comes, he is told that since he already had his one beverage, the aforementioned root beer, he is not entitled to coffee.

"What?"

"Sir, you could buy coffee?"

"Why don't I get coffee?"

"You had your drink, sir. Can I get you coffee?"

"No. I'll drink water."

"Hockey pucks, Ba, hockey pucks!" he says after the waiter goes. "A lousy cup of coffee. These miserable bastards!"

"Ach!" I say.

"Ach!" he says. "How do you not give people a lousy cup of coffee?"

How indeed!

26 September

The next day, with the Zucker Seminar pamphlet still in the car, we go to Whole Foods and Dollar Tree, the latter because "you never know what you're going to need until you get there." I'm not sure what forces within nature collide to make an octogenarian buy, count 'em, three three-liter pineapple sodas from Dollar Tree on the same day he is buying halvah from Whole Foods, but that's what he buys.

"The hell are you buying?" I ask about the soda.

"You don't get out much, do you? It's got a good taste."

"Pineapple soda from the Dollar Tree has a good taste?"

"It's refreshing. You don't know."

If I told you that, in fact, it does have a good taste, you wouldn't believe me, so let's move on. Outside Whole Food is an ASPCA Adopt-a-Puppy/Local Artists Coalition kiosk, where my father engages with a woman wearing a puppy shirt, a shirt that clearly reads "Puppy" on the front and the back.

"What do you got here for adoption — babies?" he asks.

Yes, your better adoption centers are in front of supermarkets. They just hand you a baby over the folding table.

"No, sir, puppies," she says, unamused.

"What does that say on your shirt?" he asks.

" 'Puppies.' "

"What kind of puppies?"

"All kinds."

"So we just take one?"

"Well, you have to sign up, agree to take care of the puppy, get her shots."

"Dad," I ask, "do you want a puppy?"

"No, but if they're giving them away, what the hell?" he whispers.

"They're free, Dad, yeah, but do you really want one?"

"I don't know. Eh, better not."

Near the puppies, handmade bracelets, necklaces, and rings are available on other tables.

"What kind of costume jewelry do you have here?" my father asks one of the men behind a table.

"It's not costume jewelry, sir. Local artists make what's on these tables. All custom-crafted."

"I mean, yeah, so it's . . . made?"

The man looks confused.

I'm confused.

"Sir?" he asks.

"You know," my father repeats, "the costume jewelry. It's

made . . . they make it here?" He points with his finger to this exact spot outside Whole Foods. "How often are you here?"

"About twice a month, on Saturdays."

"Oh, so about once a week?"

Samuel Beckett just got a migraine.

27 September

Took my father to see Dr. EZ Lou after his episode last week.

After telling her my father passed out, she asks about how much he drank that night.

"I had some wine," he says, "but it was just a little and I don't like wine."

Let me stop here to say that as far as my father is concerned, if you don't like the alcohol you're drinking, it doesn't count.

"How much do you drink each week?" she asks.

"Maybe three drinks a night, three times a week."

"That's nine drinks," she says, concerned.

"Yeah, but it's only gin."

You have not lived until you've seen a Nigerian doctor face-palm.

"Oh, doctor," I say, "my father told me the last time he was here, you told him to stop taking his blood pressure medicine. That didn't sound right, so I told him to keep taking it until we saw you."

"He said what?"

"That's not what you said?"

"I told him to double up on the medication because his pressure was high. It's fine now, but he should definitely stay on the Losartan."

"That's what I thought. I think from now on, I'll come with him when you want to see him."

"Maybe so. But we'll take care of Jack, I promise."

"What's that, dear?" my father asks.

"She said she is going to take care of you."

"Well, there's a lot of that going around."

"You know, Dad, that makes absolutely no sense."

On the way home — actually we're going to the casino first — my father wants a review of what the doctor said.

"What did she say about me?"

"That you're a pain in the ass."

"C'mon!"

"She said you were in great shape, and don't drink so much."

"What do I drink?"

"With the medication you're on, you should drink nothing."

"I don't drink."

"Yes, you do."

"But I don't drink that much. What else did she say?"

"That you're in great shape for a man your age."

"You're not telling me everything."

"Yes, I am. And you were right there. You heard everything."

"She didn't whisper anything to you?"

"No."

"So, tell me, Ba, why is it when we went to Italy, every station is in Italian, but in this goddamn country, I turn on the TV late at night and there are five stations in Mexican?"

My father does like moving the conversation along.

"You mean Spanish."

"In either case. I mean, you want to watch TV, those miserable bastards give you nothing to watch."

"Are you mad at Mexicans or Italians?"

"You know what I mean."

I don't.

At dinner tonight with the group, a dinner Sid buys, my father tells the waitress, "Bless you. May you never know the horrors of stretch marks." A waiter later in the evening came by, to whom my father says, "Bless you. May your harem never know the horrors of stretch marks."

See what he did there?

⁓

27 September

Jack Friedman and His Magic With the Ladies, Part the Infinity

We started off this morning at the Bagel Cafe in Summerlin.

"Barry, why did you order juice? I have juice at home."

"Dad, you have Sunny D, which is not really orange juice."

"Ah, c'mon, it's all the same."

"Dad, it's orange. That's where the similarity ends."

We then head to the Suncoast. He goes to play Crap; I go to play nickel Keno. He's smiling when we meet.

"I was flirting with the dealer," he tells me.

"How old?"

"Wait, wait. Her husband is dying of cancer, but she said he doesn't interfere with her social life. I think she wanted my number."

"What made you think that?"

"She was being very nice."

What completes the dream of "I am a dealer in Vegas, working mornings, my husband's dying, and what in God's name happened to my life?" better than the phone number of an 86-year-old man in black sweats, a blue FUBU shirt, slip-ons, and a toupee?

"Did you give her your number?"

"Nah."

"You couldn't remember your number, could you?"

"Hee-hee. You're right. I can't. What is my number, anyway?"

"If I give it to you, will you remember it?"

"Probably not."

We leave the casino and head to buy a kitchen oven, do some shopping, and then come back, because he bowls today.

⁓

27 September

The whole operation is falling apart. Apparently, a few weeks back, there was a fight at the Sunday night pinochle game at Carole's.

"I told them, Ba, I'm out and to find another player, but that I'd stick around a few weeks till they did."

Well, they found someone.

At bowling today, my father asked Lou what time the game was and Lou said his girlfriend, Vicki — Vicki Mustard, damn her! — would be taking my father's place and that the group found someone else in case Vicki couldn't always play. He was replaced, and the replacement's replacement was also lined up.

"Imagine," my dad says, "they found someone to take my place?"

"But you told them to, to be fair."

"Yeah, but pick up the phone and say something. I have to find out like this."

Agreed.

So, if you would, please join me, then, in saying to Lou, Carol, Ed, and now Vicki and the alternate, "Ya miserable bastards."

Evening Coda . . .

Tonight at dinner, without the group, I take my father to the Gold Coast Casino and to Ping Pang Pong for dinner. It's Chinese, you know. Later back at the house, we decide to watch *I, Robot*.

"What kind of a jerky picture is this?"

"I don't know."

"Put the script on the screen. Why don't they talk up?"

"You mean the subtitles?"

"No, the script."

"OK."

"Where's your mother, Barry, where's your mother?"

"She died 14 years ago. Ah, but a good question, Dad — a good question."

"She went too soon. She should have had another 10 years. He had to take her? Wouldn't have killed anybody."

30 September
The shortage of spoons is still bothering my father. This morning at breakfast at the Red Rock Buffet, he was stirring his coffee with a straw.

"There's a national spoon shortage."

"No, there's not."

"See, Ba, the spoon is the most versatile utensil, so that's why people steal them and that's why restaurants don't put them out."

"We have had this conversation before."

"When?"

"You want a date, I don't know. Anyway, what else is on your mind these days?"

"What kind of pills am I on?"

"Blood-pressure pills. In fact, we're going to see your cardiologist after breakfast."

"What? She's going to look at my heart?"

"Yes, that's what they do."

At her office, Fox News is playing in the waiting room. No wonder they do such brisk business.

"What do you do here, dear?" my father asks Dr. Barbarash when she comes in.

"Dad, this is your cardiologist. You remember her, right?"

"Oh, yeah, yeah. Just last week I was—"

"No, no, Dad," I say, "you're not telling that joke."

"What joke?"

"You know what joke."

Here's the joke he is prone to telling.

Just last week . . . I was attacking a girl in an alley and I said, "Don't scream, it's embarrassing for me too." As bad as that is, and it is, my father has mostly forgotten punchlines these days, so here's how the joke has been coming out lately: I was attacking a girl in an alley and I said, "Stand still."

Either version, as you can probably see, is not the best bit to try out on a humorless Ukrainian doctor who doesn't quite buy into the magic of Jack Friedman the way most women do. As the years went on, he'd start "Just last week . . . " I'd stop him.

"No, Dad."

"What?"

"Not that joke."

"What joke?"

"You know what joke."

"I wasn't going to tell a joke."

"Yes, you were."

"No, I swear."

OCTOBER

1 October

Leaving Vegas today and — really, this is it — this will be the last time my father is driving me to the airport. He probably shouldn't be driving anywhere, but certainly not around McCarran.

"Dad, what do you think about moving to Tulsa?"

"Tulsa? What's in Tulsa?"

"I am."

"Besides you?"

"That's it, that's the point! To be around family."

"Why?"

"Because, look, better you do it now when you can still contribute to the move, the conversation, than to have a stroke and we have to wheel you in a gurney, as you would say, 'When you don't know from nothing.' "

"I don't know, Ba."

"I know, Dad, it's tough. But you gotta think about it. I talked to Melissa and she's all for it. We'll get you a place."

"Tulsa? What's in Tulsa?"

"Dad, you need to be around family. New York, Los Angeles, or Tulsa, and Tulsa is the best place because I can spend more time with you than Wayne or Susan."

"Give me one more year. I want one more year."

How do you argue with such a clear request?

I have him stand on the curb near baggage claim so that when I hug him, I won't dwarf him. I kiss my father more and more the past few years. This moment has to be right. His stubble I remember from when I was a little boy. My sister tells me that every time she comes to see him, she thinks it will be the best time. I watch him get in the car and pull the seat closer to the steering wheel. He is wearing reading glasses he bought at Dollar Tree — the $700 ones he bought for driving aren't as comfortable or as clear, he tells me — waves, take off, nearly hitting two cars, and then drives away from Terminal One to the bowling alley at the Suncoast Casino for his Tuesday league. He will get there two hours early.

14 OCTOBER

Jack Friedman is 87 today.

I call.

"You still look good for a man your age."

"It's a rented body."

An old joke, but it still works. Told him about all the messages he's getting on Facebook from all the people he doesn't know and he was very touched . . . I think.

"That's very nice," he says. "What do you mean?"

"People write messages — it's called posting or commenting — to you about your birthday."

"Yeah. What do they say?"

" 'Happy birthday.' "

"Yeah?"

"Yeah."

"What else?"

"You want to read them?"

"Nah, just tell me. Oh, Ba, listen, I had the carpets cleaned yesterday, so from now on, people come into this house, they're going to take off their goddamn shoes. I used to make fun of people who did this, but they're right. Leave them by the door. You can take them when you leave."

How about that? My dad's letting you have your shoes back.

25 OCTOBER

Jack and Florence Friedman were married 60 years ago today. Back then, he had hair; she had it all.

NOVEMBER

11 November

I call.

"Dad, it's Veterans Day. You saved the whole damn country. On behalf of a grateful nation, I thank you."

"You're welcome. Listen, if you can't reach me, it's because I'll be eating ALL day. Breakfast, lunch, and dinner. That's right — I'm going to punish them tomorrow."

"Can you eat that much?" I ask.

"I got the comps, so what the hell?"

12 November

My father calls. He is planning another trip to Oklahoma in a few weeks.

"What's the weather like? I need to know what to pack."

"You're not coming for two weeks."

"Yeah, I know, but just generally. Will it be cold or what?"

"Well, it's, like, 50 degrees now."

"So a coat or a sweater?"

"Go with the sweater and a long-sleeve shirt."

"You know, I'll bring both."

"Good idea. Anything else new?"

"Yeah, the buffets were packed yesterday."

"There are a lot of veterans."

"Yeah, a lot of the old-timers."

19 November

The phone rings.

"What's with this computer?"

Many times we skip "Hello."

"Dad, how are you?"

"It's dead. Nothing."

"Did you turn it on?"

"What are you talking about? What do you mean, 'turn it on'?"

"The on/off button, it's in the back. Push it. See if it works."

"OK, I found it," he says, straining to stay on the phone while reaching to the back of the computer.

"Did you push it?"

"Yeah, yeah, I pushed it."

"Is it on?"

"Yeah, it's on. OK, it's working. What does it want from my life?"

"Why are you still in a bad mood? The computer is working!"

"You put a button in the back? Nu? Who puts a button in the back?"

∼

21 November

I am at the airport.

"What are you doing here?" my father asks, seeing Melissa. "You look tired. You work hard," and then, pointing to me, he adds, "unlike him."

"I can make you take a cab to our house," I say.

On the way to the house, Melissa decides to brag on me.

It did not go well.

"Jack," says Melissa, "Barry was nominated for Entertainer Entrepreneur of the Year in Tulsa and Best Columnist. It's kind of a big deal. Did he tell you?"

"Oh, yeah!" he says. "You know, I bowl with these two Filipinos."

All of which is to say, if you think you can trade non sequiturs with Jack Friedman, bring it. You will lose.

⌇

22 November

This morning, my father's friend Lou — he of the "I swear on my dead wife's grave, I don't love you" fame — called my dad and left a message, believing he had reached his doctor. One might think the outgoing message — "Hi, this is Jack, not the real Jack, so if you want to talk to the real Jack, wait for the beep and we'll talk about it" — would have alerted Lou that he was not talking to Dr. Spivak's service.

But one would be wrong.

Anyway, Lou was pissed, convinced a prescription for which he was forced to pay should have been covered by insurance, so he is calling — it is 7 a.m. on a Saturday — demanding to speak to someone, which would have been difficult even if he had been talking to someone at Dr. Spivak's office.

My father, hours later, checked his message.

"Ba, I didn't understand one word of that."

"It's Lou."

"Lou?"

"Lou."

"Who's Lou?

"Your friend Lou."

"Oh, Lou. I thought you meant someone else."

He then calls Lou.

"Lou, did you call me earlier? Hello! HELLO . . . HELLO!"

He calls back.

"Louie! Hey . . . what the . . . Hello, Lou? Hello. Anyone there?"

He calls back again.

"The guy," he says to Melissa and me, "keeps saying, 'Hello, this is not Lou' and keeps hanging up."

"Maybe it's not Lou," Melissa says, "and then the guy keeps wondering why you keep calling him back."

"I'm trying to get Lou."

"But he doesn't know that."

"These stupid phones," he says, putting it away. "I'll call Lou when I get back to Vegas."

~

23 November

Old friends of mine, Mike and Jan, always have an annual pre-Thanksgiving dinner, and that dinner was tonight. My father was invited, along with Melissa and me. Upon entering the house, we are met by Frank, an Asian man, a visiting professor from China, who has also been invited and who, incidentally, has brought spicy peanuts from his land. My father, seeing the Asian man and learning he is from China, thinks, "Hmm, I was in World War II, I fought the Japanese in the Philippines. Close enough." I know this to be the case because my dad makes the same non-distinction with his Korean nephrologist back in Las Vegas and the Vietnamese women who sometimes give him pedicures, all those places being "over there" and close to the Philippines.

My father begins to tell the Asian man with the spicy peanuts about his time in Manila and the Purple Heart he received when a piece of a bridge fell on and broke his big toe. The Asian man with the spicy peanuts smiles in a "I don't speak or understand English" kind of way.

My father then is offered and grabs a handful of the afore-mentioned nuts and pops them in his mouth.

"Wow-we-wow, they're hot!" he exclaims. "These are spicy nuts."

This makes the Asian man laugh.

At dinner, I overhear my father say to the person seated next to him, "Don't misunderstand me, I'm not devoid of sex."

24 November

My daughter, Nina, and her boyfriend, Auri, are in town as well. As mentioned, Auri is from France.

"Voulez-vous faire du shopping sur Les Champs-Élysée en Français?" my father asks Auri. And then, as best I can tell, says something about a blackbird and a hat.

He then mentions to Nina that he was seeing Vicki Schwartz — yet another Vicki, still not our favorite one — even though they broke up years ago.

"She's 20 years younger than I am. Does that make me a pedophile?"

Which, goes without saying, is a great joke to tell your grand-daughter.

We take a drive later in the day and pass Sidney Lanier Elementary School.

"Sidney Lanier?" my father asks. "Sidney Lanier?"

"Yes, Dad, Sidney Lanier."

"Out of the hills of Habersham,
Down the valleys of Hall,
I hurry amain to reach the plain,

Run the rapid and leap the fall,

Split at the rock and together again."

The man with the very bad toupee on his head and the inappropriate jokes was flawlessly reciting Sidney Lanier's Song of the Chattahoochee.

Later that night, we watch the New York Giants play the Dallas Cowboys.

"Who is this Giants quarterback? He's terrible."

When informed it's two-time Super Bowl-winning quarterback Eli Manning, my father responds, "THIS guy? C'mon! All he does is shake his head."

25 November

We also went to Bed Bath & Beyond, where a young woman named Stephany — that was her name on her name tag — was our cashier.

"Your name is spelled wrong," my father said to her. "It should be 'ie,' not 'y.' "

We then went to River Spirit, a casino owned by the Muscogee (Creek) Nation, where my father asked the valet attendant the question he thought was on everyone's mind.

"What did the Indians have here before casinos — teepees?"

26 November

Today, Jack Friedman, 87, did two crossword puzzles (for what he calls "brain exercise"), ate three meals out (including a 12-ounce sirloin and about 12 generic Oreos), went to two casinos (opposite ends of town), and watched Barabbas on the Trinity Broadcasting Network, of all networks?

"Dad, what the hell are you watching?" I asked.

"You don't know what the guy's had to go through. Oy, these Romans! They're killing everybody. Nu?"

For one of those meals, we went to lunch, and upon seeing my burrito from Chipotle, my father asked the woman behind the counter, "What is it with the people in Mexico? Everything's on a taco. You're telling me they don't know how to make a bread?"

She smiled.

Receiving his order, he said, "Thank you, Miss America, may you never know the horrors of stretch marks. Behave yourself, and if you can't, take my number."

On another drive around Tulsa, he gave us all a history of Tulsa.

"In the old days, Tulsa was a big Western town with horses and close to Texas."

～

27 NOVEMBER (DAY before Thanksgiving)

This morning my father was watching the News on 6 Now on one of the channels up the dial. An hour later, I noticed he was still watching it. The problem: It has been repeating the same news broadcast for two and a half hours. He doesn't seem to notice, much less be bothered by it. In fact, it gives him a chance every half hour or so to hear the Oklahoma Natural Gas $600 rebate report on gas dryers, which he finds astounding, as he needs a new dryer for his home in Las Vegas, even if he's not sure his dryer is electric or gas. He knows he bought it at Sears, though, which doesn't really narrow things down much. I don't know how we're going to pull this off, but pull this off we shall. Nobody denies a Friedman a rebate. Am I making myself clear? He also picked up a copy of this morning's Tulsa World.

" 'Trash board hires lawyer'? That's on the front page? What kind of news is this?"

My father also had a brief choking attack today. Luckily, he knows what caused it.

"It's those Cheerios. They make the . . . things too goddamn small. It gets stuck in your throat."

Melissa and I have a cat, Charlie, who is both an indoor and outdoor cat. When noted veterinarian Jack Friedman saw Charlie run outside, he said, "You know, the cat goes in, the cat goes out," and then, citing an exhaustive study he has in head, added, "and someday he won't come back. Yeah, they do that, these cats. It happened to somebody I know, and when they're gone, baby, they're gone."

We took another trip to Hard Rock Casino. On the casino floor, there is an autographed guitar from some rock band.

"So what the hell goes on here? You play here, you get a guitar when you leave?"

"Yes, Dad, that's exactly what happens. Everyone gets a free guitar."

28 November

Our official Thanksgiving meal is today — yesterday was spaghetti Bolognese (my father wanted something light) — which means the turkey has been cooking since about noon. First thing yesterday morning, we got in the car to do some holiday meal shopping.

"Why is the sun so goddamn strong? Is it because Oklahoma is closer to the sun?"

"Yes, Dad, I believe that's exactly why."

"What do people do in Tulsa? Is it still a money town?"

"Ah, yeah, I guess."

We arrived at Reasor's.

"So what makes it Italian food . . . the sauce?"

"Yeah, I guess."

"Tell me, Ba, Auri, Nina's boyfriend, he works at a winery. So, he works around wine?"

"Yeah."

"He likes it."

"I guess so."

"Generally, how many people at this casino right now are retired?"

"We're not at the casino."

"I mean earlier."

"I don't know."

"So what do you write, again?"

"Politics, mostly."

"Did the bird for Thanksgiving give up its life willingly or was it forced into the oven?"

"Forced?"

"What kind of name is Ree-zors . . . Jewish?"

"No, it's a guy's name — Reasor."

"So, how did the bagel get to Oklahoma?"

AT DINNER, my father decided to find out more about Auri.

"Tell me something," he asked, "is French the official language in France?"

"Yes, it is," said Auri, very patiently.

"Well, I know in the villages it probably is, but I meant in the big cities like Marseille and . . . you know, cities like that?"

Later, Thanksgiving night, we were watching television.

"Boy, she got old."

"Who?"

"Ethel Kennedy, Bobby's wife."

"She's 85, Dad."

"Yeah, but still . . . I don't remember her getting this old. Hey, where'd she go? She was just talking."

"This is now a Nationwide commercial, Dad. They were talking about her during the show that preceded this, about the Kennedys."

"Oh! Who can keep up."

≈

29 November

I took my father for a bagel at "Owl Head Bagel Cafe."

"These bagels are too voluptuous, you know, Ba. They can't be eaten by one person."

≈

30 NOVEMBER (TULSA International Airport)

Can't be at an airport with my father without thinking about turkey sandwiches, but also today, I thought of my son, Paul, when he was around two years old. My father was on the floor, talking to Paul, who was standing in his playpen, holding on to the mesh, looking out.

"Show your father what I taught you," the grandfather said to the grandson about the father and son who were watching.

I was thinking, too, of the movie *My Left Foot*. There's a scene where the father builds his son, a quadriplegic who only has use of his left foot, a room off the house, where the kid can paint, write, create. He finishes it just as the son, played by Daniel Day-Lewis, in a wheelchair and being pushed by the mother, comes home. The father passes Day-Lewis at the entrance to the new room and puts his hand on his son's shoulder, just for a second, and then keeps walking.

"Well, Christy," says the mom to the son, pointing to the room and the father, "that's the nearest he'll ever come to saying he loves you."

And, yeah, I made my father a turkey sandwich for the flight home today, because, you know, those "miserable bastards give you nothing to eat on the plane."

"Got any of the bird left?" he asked this morning on the way to the airport.

"Yeah, I'll make you something to eat for the trip."

"OK, great!"

"Like before, right?"

"Yeah! Yes, yes, yes! But ketchup this time."

"What about the mustard? You made such a big thing about mustard last time."

"Eh, ketchup's better."

DECEMBER

14 December

My father called. Someone in "the Mob" had disappointed him.

"So the guy wants to be like that? Fine. I'm not going to play his shit-ass game. I pick up plenty of checks. Plenty! You know, Ba, all this talk about senior citizens and what have you about this and that — it's not true. Old people are not good. They're not good."

22 December

I am planning a trip to Vegas. I got a week's work at Sin City.

"Ba," he says on the phone, "when you get here, we'll go to this Italian place. We'll make a major purchase. I think I need a new printer. It doesn't print."

"Maybe it's just a cartridge."

"Nah, let's make a major purchase."

In the past, there is always one expensive thing we buy — television, cell, tires, something. He seems to enjoy doing so.

"Also, we'll go this Italian place. The food's great, but the portions are enormous, so here's what we'll do: We'll order one veal parmesan and split it. OK with you?"

"Yeah, fine."

"Because the portions are way too big. Way too big. You can't eat it by yourself."

"Well, I probably could, but whatever you think."

"No, we can order two, if you think, but I'm just telling you they're too big."

"Then order one."

"I think we should."

"That's fine."

"I mean, I don't know. What the hell, maybe we'll order two."

Glad that's settled.

24 DECEMBER (LAS VEGAS)

I'm in Vegas. We're at the bowling alley.

"Yeah, Jesus came from a Jewish family," he tells Lou.

Lou, a practicing Christian, does not seem to be enjoying this liturgical moment.

"Huh?"

"Yeah, Mary and Joe Schwartz were his parents. And then he grew up and converted to Christianity."

Lou went to pick up a spare.

Later in the day.

"So, Ba, how does Melissa celebrate Christmas?"

"By celebrating Christmas."

"You mean with presents and the whole mishpocha ["family" in Yiddish]?"

"Yeah, a lot of mishpocha in southwest Kansas."

"Nice."

30 DECEMBER

My father called to tell me that Dana, my cousin, is a lawyer but also a professional Santa Claus. Dana's father, my father's middle brother, Hy, died about 20 years ago.

"My brother would have killed him."

31 DECEMBER

My father calls.

"Hey, Ba, I'm going over to Jennifer's tonight and I'm probably going to spend the night."

"Jennifer?"

"You met her."

"Do you mean Jeannette, your girlfriend?"

"Yeah, what did I say?"

"Jennifer?"

"I mean Jeannette."

"I met her many times."

"I forgot."

"No, I know her."

"She's a good girl. Doesn't like me driving home late at night. She's buried two husbands, you know."

3

2014

This was the year — I knew when it started — I was going to get my father out of Las Vegas. This was going to be the year he asked for.

He was 88 and playing, as they say in these parts, "with house money."

His friend Bill had called me a couple of times in the past six months. I'd see his name on caller ID and know it was not going to be good.

"I do what I can, Barry," he told me in a call once, "but I think he needs to be closer to you, your brother or sister. I sure will miss him, but I think it'll be better this way. I wish I had somewhere to go to be closer to family, but I don't."

Bill's wife, Cynthia, had Alzheimer's and it was progressing pretty rapidly.

"I have begged her family to come help me, take her back to Indiana," he said, "because I can't do it all."

Bill has not been in the best shape either, so he knew there would come a point where he'd have to institutionalize her — and listening to him talk about having to watch her, clean up after her, make sure she didn't set the house on fire, I couldn't help but wonder . . . if that time was now.

"You ever talk to her?" my father would ask me every so often about Cynthia.

"Yeah, why?"

"It's like she's not even there. Sometimes she knows who I am, sometimes she doesn't."

Alzheimer's, I heard once, is not when you put your keys in the refrigerator — it's when you forget what the keys and refrigerator do. My father had already been in two car accidents — neither, he insisted, his fault, even though moments before the second one, he had fallen asleep behind the wheel before running the car into a steel construction cord that somehow attached itself to the underside of the car and literally yanked it (and him) off the ground. I was in the Bahamas during the first week of January in 2014 when this happened. I got an email, not a call, from the insurance company the morning after the accident to inform me that it knew of the accident and was proceeding with the claim.

"You all right?" I asked my father when I called.

"What?"

"What? What do you mean, 'What'? You had an accident?"

"How did you hear?"

"Got an email."

"From who?"

"The insurance company."

"Why are they telling you?"

"Because I'm contacted in case anything happens to you."

"You? Why you?"

"You want someone else?"

"I'm not knocking it. I'm just curious."

"Yeah, me."

"Why'd they tell you?"

"They wrote there was an accident. What happened?"

"I was upside down, Ba. I must have dozed."

"You fell asleep?"

"Well, I dozed."

"Interesting distinction. Go on."

"I don't know. I woke up, I'm in the car, I'm almost upside down. I hit something."

"Were you hurt?"

"No."

"What time did this happen?"

"About 11 in the morning."

"You feel asleep at 11 in the morning behind the wheel?"

"I didn't fall asleep. I dozed."

"Fine."

"I had taken an Ambien around five because I hadn't been sleeping well, so maybe that had something to do with it."

"I'm thinking it definitely had something to do with it."

"Anyway, the car's totaled, so I'll need another one."

"Did you go to the hospital?"

"No."

"How'd you get home?"

"I called Bill."

"Don't buy a car until I get there."

He did.

By the time I arrived in Vegas after the Bahamas gig was over, he already had his new Honda Civic.

"How long did this take you to buy?" I asked.

"I think I went last week sometime. I needed wheels. C'mon, we have to go back there for lube and service."

"Lube and service? Who told you it needed that?"

"Lube and service, you know."

"I know the term, but this car doesn't need it. It's a week old."

"These cars, you got to take them for lube and service, that's all."

"Please stop saying 'lube and service.' "

"It needs oil, then."

"Not now it doesn't."

"What about the wheels?"

"The wheels? You mean the tires?"

"Yeah, the tires."

"The tires are fine."

We went to the Honda dealer.

The guy at the dealership who sold him this car — and I knew it was the guy because my father pointed him out to me when we arrived — was sitting in front of the dealership on the window ledge with a bunch of other guys. They all had on windbreakers, eyeglasses with transitional lens, and creased beige slacks. All they needed was to be sitting in front of a Satriale's Pork Store sign.

"Can I help you?" my father's salesman asked.

He had no idea who my father was.

"I need lube and service," my father said.

"Oh, for Chrissakes," I muttered.

"What?" the guy asked.

"You know, lube and service."

"Sir, the car doesn't . . . tell you what, take it back to the service bay. They'll help you out."

I have no idea what they did, but it was $119.

As 2013 WAS the first concerted year of this diary of my life with my father, I was amazed about those who started following along. It wasn't just the numbers of people, though that was flattering, but mostly it was the knowledge, retention, and interest of those who did so. My rabbi in Tulsa called me and referred to "poor Jeannette"; Charlie Pierce of Esquire called my father's mahjongg group "miserable bastards" for excluding him; Atlantic magazine's Garrett Epps, Slate's Dahlia Lithwick, and others checked in daily about whether there was any elucidating on how Bernie died. Dahlia referred to my father as "America's Comedy Dad," which seemed about right. While the conversations were unfolding, I would start thinking about the posts I'd write.

~

JANUARY

~

11 JANUARY

The phone rings.

"Barry, it's Dad."

(Sometimes it was Barry; sometimes it was Ba. Hilarious to me was the " . . . it's Dad" part. Once when my mother was alive, he called and said, "Ba, have you seen Florence?")

"I know it's you."

"What?"

"I know it's you."

"How's Melissa?"

"She has the flu, slight fever, stomachache. Really not doing well."

"Hey, it's no joke — this flu. Listen, I went bowling yesterday. Bowled terribly. Couldn't make a spare to save my ass."

Something about bowling brought out the non sequitur in him.

~

ON THE WEEKS I wasn't in Las Vegas, I would talk to him three or four times a week. Sometimes multiple times per day. I was on his automatic dialer, which helped as the years went on, though well into his nineties he always remembered my phone number. He remembered this one, too: "GE6-9328. That's 212 area code." That was his home telephone number when he lived at 922 57th Street in Brooklyn . . . in 1940.

15 January

DURING TODAY'S PHONE CALL:

"See, Ba, most older people are subservient to their children because the younger people think the older people don't know what the fuck they're doing, so they take over from them. And that's why the older people are so conflicted. Anyway, I have a persona, so I'm not yielding."

"OK, I never thought you were conflicted. You conflicted?"

"Conflicted?"

"You said conflicted."

"What do you mean?"

"I don't know what you meant."

"All right, listen, we have a Smith's nearby that has an enormous kosher section, and I'm not a kosher person, but I'm going to go anyway and schmooze around."

"Sounds good."

17 JANUARY

~

MY FATHER CALLS.

"What does this stupid computer want from my life?"

"What's the matter?"

"Where does the disc go?"

"What disc?"

"The disc."

"OK, the disc," I say, though I don't know what disc. "Dad, what disc?"

"The disc!"

"You have to give me more."

"The disc!"

"The disc? Ah — TurboTax?"

"Yes. Where's the goddamn disc?"

"Push the 'eject' button on the keyboard."

"The what?"

"The thing you type on. There should be a button."

"I pushed that."

"Did the little drawer open?"

"Yes."

"Is the disc in there?"

"Let me look again."

I hear him tapping the keyboard.

"You miserable bastard."

"You found it?"

"It was in there."

"So what do you want to do now?"

"No, I was just looking for it."

"Well, there it is. Now you have to put it in the computer."

"What do you mean?"

"In the computer itself."

"So what do I do?"

"Put it back in the tray and close it."

"There's no hole for the disc."

"Just place it in the tray and then push the button to close it."

"Does the TurboTax label face me or away?"

"Dad . . . "

"Wait, I see 2012. Where the hell's 2013? . . . What kind of download? I DOWNLOADED IT! Where the hell is it? It keeps telling me to download. I did it 14 times already."

"Dad—"

"—application folder? What do you mean, 'application folder'? Screw it! I'm going bowling."

"That's the spirit—"

"Technology . . . oy! Why is Madigan's 2010 return coming up?" [Madigan was a tax client of his.]

" . . . I don't want Safari. Who hit Safari? Where's the fakakta icon? It was just there. Now it's all gone."

"You don't really need me for this phone call, do you?"

"I'm going to put my foot through this goddamn computer. Now I got five icons. Which ones can I get rid of? You know what? I'm not touching any of them. Ba, look, I'm not really a computer person."

"Go bowling, Dad."

"I'm going to go bowling."

∾

25 JANUARY

He calls.

"Ba, I just got a letter from the Coumadin Clinic — saying my INR level, whatever the hell that is — is 2.1, and now I'm at the Suncoast, where the guy says to me — Nu? He says to ME! I don't have to ask — 'Take a break and here's a comp. Go eat something.' And I'm coming to you in September, right?"

The amount of ground my father can cover in one conversation is astonishing.

FEBRUARY

17 FEBRUARY

I'm here at his house on Tumble Brook Drive for the week, and during the breakfast buffet at the Suncoast today, he told me for the 356th time that Jennifer, his present girlfriend [her name is Jeannette], is from Vermont, she lives in a trailer, and has buried two husbands, Ba.

"Imagine! Two!"

"Dad, I know. You've told me this."

"I have?"

"Yeah."

"I don't remember."

"But imagine: two husbands. Yeah, so Sunday I was playing over at Carole's."

"You're playing pinochle again?"

"Yeah, yeah. That's all softened."

"Good. Glad you're all getting along again."

"So, Carole, you know Carole, right?"

"Yeah."

"Her husband. He had a jeep fall on him during the war."

"Ouch!"

"Don't knock it. He's got a great pension."

"You think it was worth it?"

"What?"

"Nothing."

"But he and Carole don't have sex."

"Too bad."

"She told me, 'Jack, I'm so dry, so you can't have me either.' "

"She had a way with men, don't you think?"

"Ah, Ba, where's your mother? Where's your mother? I bet she's looking and thinking, 'Jack, so where the hell are you already?' She was so goddamn good-looking, your mother."

And we hadn't even slid into lunch yet.

At lunch, however, at the Bagel Cafe on North Buffalo, he was somewhat taken aback by the extent of the Jewish diaspora.

"You know, Ba, Savas, who owns this place, is Greek — a real Greek, no joke — and he married a Jewish girl. Imagine: a Greek and a Jew."

"That's not so strange — we Jews are allowed to marry anyone these days."

"No, my point is, he married a Jew and he's Greek."

"Got it."

Just then he saw someone he recognized.

"See that guy over at the counter?"

"Yeah."

"I think his name is Phil. I see him a lot in here. Jewish guy, from Ohio. Very religious guy. Who knew they had Jews in Ohio?"

"They're all over the place."

"This place does big business with Jews," he tells me. "On weekends, the place is mobbed. All Jews."

18 FEBRUARY

It's Tuesday, which means it's bowling, and also, not that we need one, another chance to eat out. But first, a little flirtation with Jade, the 20-something cashier at Einstein Bros Bagels.

"How goes your life, Miss America?"

"Fine, Jack. How are you?"

Apparently they know each other.

"Got a half hour, I'll tell you the whole story. Better yet, wait for the movie, it's in color. It's a porno flick. You'll like it."

The man is relentless.

Nervous laughter from Jade.

"You got some water, dear? I need to take a pill. It makes me horny."

Jesus!

"I'm kidding, I'm kidding. Just last week I was attacking a girl in a dark alley and I said, 'Please don't scream. It's embarrassing for me, too, you know.'"

Yeah, he told it again. And Jade has heard it.

"You're impossible," she says.

"OK, behave yourself. And if you can't, take my number. But some water, dear. Please."

At the Suncoast Lanes, he was talking to the very religious Lou.

"So he was Jewish, his parents were Jewish, Mary and Joe Schwartz . . . whatever, and then, as Jesus got older, he converted to Christianity. Besides, what kind of immaculate conception? They were married, Joseph and Mary. You mean they never had sex? C'mon! And what kind of husband lets his pregnant wife ride on a mule?"

20 FEBRUARY

This morning, my father and his Honeywell HomMed Health Monitoring System — which not only tracks his vitals, blood pressure, pulse, weight, etc., but sends the information to Dr. EZ Lou — had a conversation.

"Please step on the scale," the machine ordered at precisely the time we set it to have him do this.

"All right, give me a minute," my father says, sitting in the living room.

"Please step on the scale," the machine "says" again.

"I'm coming, you hockey puck."

"Please step on the scale."

"I'm coming, I'm coming."

"Please step on the scale."

"Give me a minute, for crying out loud!"

"Please step on the scale."

He arrives in the kitchen.

"I'm on it, I'm on it."

"Please step off the scale."

"Get on the scale, get off the scale. What a nudge!"

"Please insert your arm into the cuff as instructed by your physician."

"No, I won't. Talk to my lawyer."

"Please insert your finger into the finger slot."

"Ha. I'll give you a finger."

"Please insert your finger into the finger slot."

"All right, it's in, it's in."

"Please remove your finger from the finger slot."

"ALL RIGHT! Jesus!"

"Please continue to take your medication as prescribed by your doctor and continue a healthy lifestyle."

"No, I won't."

"Goodbye."

"Talk to you tomorrow."

Later that day, at dinner, my father once again shows off his magic with the ladies.

"Do you have Half & Half?" he asks the waitress.

"Yes, we do," says the waitress.

"Oooh, oooh, it's better than sex. If you did windows, I'd marry you."

"I'll get you some."

"Bless you, my dear. May you never know the horrors of stretch marks."

The act isn't old if you haven't heard it.

Later that day, we're in a gift shop at Bally's.

"So, we're in the Philippines," he says to me, like I've never heard the story, "holding sections of a bridge, and we hear bombs. The sergeant says, 'Drop the bridge and run,' so I run, but the wrong way and I don't let go of the bridge. The last thing I hear is 'You're running the wrong way . . . kaboom!' Anyway, then I look down and see my boot is cut, so I take it off, along with my sock, and I see the nail on the big toe is gone and I see blood. I then pass out. And when I wake up in the hospital, I go to the bathroom, when I come back there's a Purple Heart on my bed.

The cut boot . . . the nail. All new to me.

"Say, Dad, where's the medal now?"

"Who knows? It's around. Hey, can I get one of those Veteran license plates?" he asks, pointing to a display of them on the gift shop wall.

"Yeah, of course you can."

"Are they free?"

"No, they're not free."

"Why aren't they free? I served my country. I won the war."

"Good point. These miserable bastards. Give the veterans a free license plate. We should go bitch to the cashier."

21 FEBRUARY

I'm still at his house on Tumble Brook. One morning, he goes out to play tennis, four-game sets with the Jewish pilot, when four shirts arrive from a company called Haband. One teal, one black, one Hawaiian, one more of a Rorschach test: starbursts, stripes, half moons, and what appear to be tiny menorahs strategically placed throughout.

"Dad, wow! Just wow!" I say to him when he gets home.

"I love these shirts so," he says.

"Why?"

"What do you know about fashion? Look at you. The jeans and the cotton shirt hanging out. Is that how they dress in Oklahoma? If so, I'm not coming."

"Hey, what watch is that?" I ask, noticing something amiss. "Where's the Movado we got you?"

"I put it away. It stopped working."

"Maybe it just needs a battery. So what's this watch?"

"It came free with the shirts."

"No, it didn't."

"Not this order — an earlier one."

Later . . . heading to the Red Rock Casino, after dinner with "the Mob," Ed is complaining about the "bleeding hearts," Ivan is talking about Hiroshima, Lou is explaining his really good deal on a Nissan Murano, and my father chimes in, but not before nearly choking on a piece of romaine.

"Why are there so many goddamn mattress stores? Every corner! What, they're short? They wear them out faster in Las Vegas?"

"Hey, Dad, let me ask you. And we'll get back to the mattresses, I promise. But Sol and Muriel [two other sometime members of "the Mob"] . . . they're married, right?"

"Yeah, I think. I mean, I don't know. Married? Maybe. Why?"

"Is she always so unfriendly to you? She was downright mean."

"Well, you know, she's Jewish, he's Italian. And I don't know if she's unfriendly. No, I mean, she's cold, but I don't think unfriendly. And she doesn't bowl, either."

22 FEBRUARY

Earlier this week, my father and I had lunch with my old

comedy booker Kevin Kearney at Ping Pang Pong. It's the Chinese place, if I haven't mentioned it. Today we saw Kevin again, and my father told him the exact joke Kevin told him at lunch.

"A woman wins the lottery and a reporter asks, 'What are you going to do now?' "

"Take a milk bath."

"Pasteurize?"

"No. Just up to my tits."

23 FEBRUARY

Jack Friedman's Magic with the Ladies, Rosa Edition.

"I think my cleaning lady wants to marry me," he tells me after Rosa, his cleaning lady, finishes cleaning his house.

"Why do you say that?"

"You should see how she kisses and hugs me when she comes over. An attractive woman, too. No joke."

"How old is she?"

"Late thirties, forties, fifties, maybe sixties . . . older. I don't know."

"That's a big gap, Dad. You might want to get that nailed down."

"Yeah, well, what are you going to do? I gave her a key."

"She cleans your place — that's a good thing."

"Well, she's got it. I told her to come over anytime."

"Smooth."

MARCH

2 MARCH

Last time I was in Vegas, I installed Skype on my father's computer.

"So, Dad, look, when I call, the computer will ring like this," I said, calling from my cell, "and then you hit the Skype icon here" — I showed him — "and then the video pops up on the screen. We can talk and see each other."

"I know, I know, I know," he said.

"No, you don't."

"I do."

"You sure?"

"Yeah, yeah, yeah, hit the button and . . . I know."

Today, I call. I hear his computer ring, followed by a swoosh, clicking, some banging.

"What the hell is going on?" I hear him say.

"Dad!"

"TurboTax? What the hell is TurboTax doing here? I want to check a balance."

"Dad, it's Barry."

"Jerry Wisotsky? I don't want his return. Who asked for his return?"

"Dad!"

"It's from 2012."

"Dad!"

"Barry?"

"What are you doing?"

"Barry? Where are you? Now the computer is frozen up. What the hell is going on?"

"Dad!"

"Barry? Where are you?"

"In the Bahamas."

"Are you on the home phone or the cell? What the hell is ringing?"

"I'm talking to you on the computer."

"What? Let me get to the other phone—"

"No, no—"

"Listen, let me ask you: Why is this thing frozen up? I can't do anything. I can't get rid of TurboTax."

"Click the 'video' button."

"What? Where are you? All I'm seeing is the pier."

"That's your background. Quit TurboTax."

"What?"

"Quit . . . never mind, we'll just talk. How are you?"

"Going to Laughlin tomorrow. Five bucks, you get the bus, they buy you lunch. Wait, I think it went up to 10. Everything's cool. I'm just looking to check my balance."

"Feeling OK?"

"Yeah, yeah, where are you?"

"I'm—"

"—Yeah, yeah, cold is subsiding. Pressure's good. Won some money last night, but now I can't do a goddamn thing on this computer. I didn't do anything, I swear. I haven't been on it all week."

"Don't worry about it."

"Why can't I get rid of this return? Who asked for Wisotsky's 2012 return?"

"Look, I'm going to go. Just shut the computer down. Pull the plug if you have to."

"Where's the plug?"

"In the back."

[Pause]

"There's no plug."

"There's a plug."

"There's no plug, I'm telling you."

"There's a plug."

"Where?"

"In the back."

"In the back of what?"

"The computer."

"Oh, oh, I see it, OK—"

I assume he successfully unplugged the computer: The call went dead.

3 March

I called again today from the Bahamas. I tried Skype again. He answered once, said hello, and hung up. I called back. He hung up without saying hello. Eventually, he answered with video — well, half video, no audio. I just saw the top of the toupee — the brown one.

He called back. Somehow he did it on Skype. He was half visible, but there was audio. A toupee was talking to me.

"What the fuck is going on with this machine? I can't do a goddamn thing. It asks me for my email address, I give it. . . . Nothing. Miserable bastard!"

"Dad—"

"Let me go. I'll call you back."

∼

5 March

In which Jack Friedman, still wrestling with Skype, brags a little and gives me a taste of his planned TED speech, titled "Bringing the 21st-Century World to Old Jews."

I call. He appears. All of him. It looks, though I can't be certain, like there's a new toupee.

"What I found with Skype," he says, "it's easy when you know what you're doing. Before I didn't know. Now I do. Much of technology is like that. You just have to know what the hell's going on."

∼

7 March

I call from the Bahamas.

"Why did you call on the home phone?" he asks. "Use Skype. It's easier."

"Did you really just say that? You?"

"Nah, it's better this way. I'm doing a return on TurboTax and I can never get back to it when I'm on Skype. What's up, sweetheart? The comedy club doing the business down there or what? How's the gate?"

My good friend Scott Dickensheets, editor of Desert Companion magazine, called today as well and asked if on my next trip out to Vegas I would keep a diary of my time with my father for publication.

Oh, absolutely.

～

27 March

I'm back in Tulsa.

He calls.

"Hey, Ba, I'm out of black ink. I need black ink for the color job, you know, the color printer. I need black. Not the colors, just the black. Can you order me five or six?"

"Yeah, sure. What are you doing up?"

"Knocking out some returns — feeling good, pressure's good. Got a lot of money coming in. And the black's coming out blue, so I need black. I mean, I can do without it, but order me five or six, OK?"

"Why do you need five or six?"

"What?"

"Why do you — never mind. I'll get them."

"Did I wake you? You up?"

"It's fine. Wait, why are you printing on the color job? You have three laser printers."

"Yeah, they're working fine. But it's good to have a spare."

. . .

APRIL 2014

4 APRIL

He calls.

"Ba, this stupid computer is frozen, my phone's not working. I mean, it's working but you can't use it, and I got black ink all over the desk. I must have put it in upside down after I shook it up. I mean, the ink."

"Why did you shake it up?"

"Aren't you supposed to?"

"No."

"Anyway, let's get a new printer when you come out."

"OK."

Ever since he moved to Las Vegas, in his apartment on South Pavilion and at the house on Tumble Brook Drive, he would call with such requests. He would never buy a printer without me, or make any electronics purchase without me — or, for that matter, any purchase more than, say, $50 — except maybe a Honda Civic I think he enjoyed the company and I looked forward to such trips to Best Buy, the Apple Store, even Target. Had I a real job — and most people in my life reminded me that I didn't — these years with my father and all these trips would have been impossible. Often, he'd call and say, "Ba, come out, we'll schmooze around and make a major purchase." My girl-friend, Melissa, was always understanding about me leaving for a week or two, even if they entailed — and usually only entailed — plugging in his computer, fixing his broken eyeglasses, buying him another electric razor, or simply sliding into buffets with him. The razors were the most maddening. He'd never clean them, so when the hair from his stubble filled up the chamber, he'd remove the floating heads and invariably lose one or break it putting it back together. Thing is, he'd never let me throw the old ones out ("I'll keep it for a spare. It's good to have spares").

"Oh, one more thing," he says. "I can't get online. I'm looking at the thing you told me about. Two lights. Supposed to have four, right?"

"Did you call Century Link?"

"Forty-five times I called. They put me on hold for a half hour and then I do what they tell me to do and nothing happens. I turn it on, I turn it off. Nothing. I mean, I don't need the online, just to check bank balances. But it's annoying."

"Well, you need the online to check your balances."

"They come in the mail. But I print them anyway."

"I don't know why you do that."

"I like to see them, that's all."

"All right, but you can keep them online and just check every day to make sure nothing's gone wrong."

"You know, the hell with it. Technology has a mind of its own. I'm going bowling. If you need to reach me, leave the message on the cell because the stupid home phone's not working, did I tell you?"

"You mentioned it. I'll fix that next time I see you. You know, Dad, you never pick up your cell."

"That's because I can't hear the goddamn thing. I think I need a new phone. Next time you come out here."

10 APRIL

7:59 a.m. CST, the phone rings.

"I stopped taking the goddamn Celebrex."

"What? Who told you to do that?"

"Were you sleeping?"

"Doesn't matter."

"I did. And let me tell you something: I feel much better. These doctors don't know shit."

"Dad, listen, you should really continue taking it because it's not good to stop taking medication cold turkey. And the Celebrex helped you, didn't it?"

"Oh, yeah, it did."

"So why'd you stop taking it?"

"I don't know. It was annoying me."

"Annoying you?"

"Yeah, what am I taking it for?"

"For your aches and pains. You have arthritis."

"Who does?"

"You do."

"I do?"

"You do."

"Yeah, I know."

"It was helping, right?"

"Yeah."

"So keep taking it."

"Yeah, you're right. I'll keep taking it."

"How long have you stopped? I mean, how long have you been off it?"

"Just since this morning."

∾

13 APRIL

In which we are reminded that Jack Friedman doesn't dwell. He calls.

"Where did it all go, Ba, where did it all go?"

"Who knows? Good thing it's still going, though, huh?"

"Oh, I went to Jennifer's earlier. She made a pot roast."

"Jeannette."

"Yeah."

"You said Jennifer."

"I mean Jessica."

"Jeannette."

"Ah, Jeannette."

∾

16 APRIL

Las Vegas

I need to preface this. Last year, I made contact with one of my favorite sportswriters, Jerry Izenberg. As a teenager, my best friend, Dave, and I used to sit in his basement in Green-lawn, New York, and watch Izenberg on a show called Sports Extra on Channel 5 on Sunday nights. Jerry semiretired, even-tually, and was living in Henderson, Nevada, when I inter-viewed him for a story I was writing for Desert Companion. After the piece came out, Jerry decided I was worthy enough — and I think those were his exact words — and we used to meet at a coffee shop at the Grand Cafe at the Sunset Station Casino in Henderson for lunch. Old cranky Jews in coffee shops — I can't recommend it enough. I'd listen to Jerry's stories about Muhammad Ali, the Democratic National Convention of 1968, where he got his wrist broken, and where he yelled at Eugene McCarthy. The man knew America, knew sports.

"I should charge you fucking tuition just to talk to me," he once said to me.

Anyway, I had decided I should bring my father, 87, and Jerry, 83, together. It would be 170 years of kvetching in a coffee shop. Moments like this do not happen often enough in life.

"How goes your life?" my father asks Jerry while I introduce them near the revolving dresser display.

"Don't ask," Jerry says.

"I'm pushing 90."

"I'm 83."

"You behaving yourself?"

"Of course not. You?"

"Got a half hour? I'll tell you the whole story. Or you can wait for the movie. It's in color."

"No, I don't," says Jerry, smiling.

"You'll hear from my lawyer about this, as soon as he gets out of jail," my father calls after him as Jerry walks way.

Great part of that: Jerry wasn't doing well at the time (he has since recovered), so I tell my dad to have a seat at the counter because I want to walk Jerry to his car. I reach Jerry in the casino.

"What are you doing?" Jerry asks, seeing me.

"Walking you to your car."

"Why?"

"You're an old Jew in pain, that's why."

"Ach! Go back to your father."

"Jerry—"

"Go back to your father," he said, raising his voice filled with love. "I'll be fine."

17 April

Las Vegas

In which Jack Friedman screams in Yiddish at a crossword puzzle he believes is treating him unfairly.

"Ver iz das, ver iz das! Who is this? David Bowie's wife? Who's David Bowie? He's got a wife? Who cares? . . . 'Magma'? What does this guy [crossword puzzle guy] want from my life? . . . 'Turns turtle'? I give up, Ba, I give up. This fakakta puzzle!"

At which point, still in his blue robe, he heads into the living room, lies down on his sofa, turns on the television, finds the music station, and proceeds to fall asleep during Kuhlau's "Flute Quintet No.3."

Later that same day, on our way to an afternoon buffet, he alerts me to a relationship dealbreaker.

"Maybe I'll get married again."

"You're 87. Why do you want to do that?"

"I don't know. Why not? Who should I marry?"

"How about Jeannette?"

"Not Jewish."

"What do you care?"

"I want a Jewish girl! It doesn't matter if she goes to shul or not. The religion, I don't care about that. Besides, she's Christian."

"She's Catholic, right?"

"Whatever she is . . . I don't know. She crosses herself."

"So?"

"I don't want a girl who crosses herself."

DINNER with the Mob has been moved to Thursday night. I think it's at Carrabba's Italian Grill.

"Hey, Dad, where we going tonight, what are we looking for?"

"I think it's called Barabbas."

Carrabba's . . . Barabbas. Close enough.

At dinner, Jeannette is once again angry with him and not sitting with him.

"What did you do, Dad?"

"I didn't do nothing! I come in, say hello, and she gives me the wave-off."

"The 'wave-off' sounds serious."

"Ach, I need this?"

"C'mon! What did you do? You did something."

"Nothing, I swear. I think she wants me to call more. I'm not a caller."

"Hey, Jack," whispers Lou, who's across the table, "you paying for Jeannette's dinner?"

"Not tonight," my father says. "She's sitting way over there."

18 April

"Dad, I'm going out for trash bags."

"Why?"

"You've got a 20-gallon bag in a container that needs a 39-gallon."

"No, I don't."

"Would I lie about something like this?"

"Yes, you would!"

"I would?"

"Yes!"

"OK, that's hilarious. Seriously, I'm going out for the bags."

"C'mon, I don't have that much garbage. I eat out most of the time."

"Why are you arguing with me about this? You have a kitchen trash bag in a garbage pail. Trust me on this."

"All right, all right. Go. Don't forget. Get the 39-gallon ones. The ones I have in there don't fit."

19 April

My father, stay with me here, loves pineapple soda. And in case you're wondering, yes, it is very much a thing. Even odder, my father is quite the devotee of three-liter pineapple soda from Dollar Tree. (Please take a moment to, you should pardon the expression, drink all that in.) Imagine my concern, then, when opening the refrigerator this morning (and, yes, I'm still here), across from the two containers of fat-free French vanilla coffee creamer and a bottle of pinot gris, I see a two-liter bottle of something called Pineapple Passionfruit Soda, a rust-and-lime-colored beverage, next to the aforementioned regular pineapple brand.

"The hell, Dad?" I ask, bringing him the bottle of passionfruit.

"I couldn't find my pineapple soda, so I bought this."

"But there's a bottle of regular pineapple in there as well."

"I bought that somewhere else."

"So you made two trips to two dollar stores for pineapple-themed sodas?"

"Yeah, the first dollar store was sold out of the regular pineapple."

"Hard to imagine."

"I'll knock you on your ass."

"What does it taste like? Because it looks like antifreeze."

"I like it! Leave me alone."

"Passionfruit, huh?"

"Jesus Christ, it's my soda. That's it! You can't have any. It's mine!"

Later that day, we discuss potluck-dinner protocol as we enter Costco. Jeannette has invited us to her complex at 5 p.m. for dinner. I have been to her clubhouse once before for one of these. Last time, a guy in a white suit brought a karaoke machine and people danced.

"Dad, I'm telling you, we need to bring something tonight."

"No, we don't. People bring things. You know — salads. There will be plenty of food. What is it with Costco? Five thousand pounds of this, 5,000 pounds of that, but you can't find a lousy box of corn flakes. What do they want from my life? By the way, we have to pick up Bill and Ralph at quarter to four."

My father can't remember Cynthia's name. (If you're asking why "Ralph," you don't know Jack about Jack.)

"How many times are you going to tell me this?"

"I'm just telling you: quarter to four. Don't get shook up."

"Now, back to the potluck dinner—"

"No, no, no, I'm telling you: People will be bringing salads and whatnot."

"Yes, and we are people, so we need to bring something."

"No, we don't. There will be salads there. Listen to me!"

"Again with the salads."

Serendipitously, Bill calls me during this time to say he's bringing red wine and that we should bring white. I return to my father, who's holding a large box of granola.

"Who can eat this much? People think they're saving money because they buy in bulk."

"People ARE saving money because they buy in bulk."

"They are? Where do you get your information?"

"Listen, Bill just called me."

"On the phone? Here? You mean on the cell?"

"Yeah."

"Don't forget to remind me: We need to pick them up at quarter to four."

Astonishing.

"Anyway, he's bringing something tonight, red wine, and said we should bring white wine."

"Yes, yes, good idea. Let's get some."

20 APRIL

If my father had a "Greatest Hits Collection," this would be on it. The other night at dinner, the potluck dinner, around a room full of people, he reminds people of the Jesus and Joe Schwartz story.

"Yes, yes, we gave you a god. Mary and Joe Schwartz couldn't find a room at the inn, so they put them in a barn. Now, remember, Christ was Jewish, technically, so he had to convert from Judaism to Catholicism and then you formed a religion around him. But it doesn't make sense. Because if Mary's a virgin, it doesn't coincide. How can you be a virgin and give birth? No good, baby."

It being April just adds to the beauty of the story being told.

21 APRIL

In which Jack Friedman destroys the game

"Golf! Golf?" my dad asks as we drive past a patch of green (not a golf course) on the way to the breakfast buffet at the Suncoast Casino.

He is in the passenger seat.

"We live in a desert. Trees they plant. And golf courses. Nu? People stand around to hit a ball into a cup and are paid a million dollars. This is a sport? They hit a ball in a tiny cup and then get in a cart and drive to where the ball is."

Let me just interrupt here to say my father actually mimics the driving of the cart. He has the "steering wheel" up to his face.

"Then they get out, someone hands them a club," and here he mimics the handing off of this club in slow motion, "and then they hit the ball again, and get back in the cart. This is the most — what do I say . . . uh, athletic . . . physical . . . you know, whatever — I've ever seen. And why? To get the drink at the end. Always the drink at the end. That's golf! 'What'd you do all day, honey?' 'Well, I tried to hit a ball in a cup and then we drank when it was over. And I got a million dollars.' "

22 APRIL

For days now, there has been a pungent smell coming from the kitchen. I noticed it when I arrived last week, but it's been getting worse. I've been looking unsuccessfully, but then, in the cabinet reserved for small pots, I discovered a bag of potatoes, soft potatoes with sprouts coming out, sitting in a pan. Worse, behind that was another bag of potatoes, even older. I know this because its contents had reverted to their liquid form and leaked all over the inside of the cabinet, resulting in a potato liquid sheen on his pretty blue shelf paper.

"Hey, Dad, what are you making in here, potato whiskey?"

"What are you talking about?"

"You got everything but the still. You can make moonshine."

He comes to look.

"You know, I thought I smelled something."

He then starts spraying the area with potpourri and strawberry air freshener.

"Tell you what, you go sit, let me really clean out the cabinet, change the shelf paper, OK?"

He keeps spraying.

"Dad, go!"

He goes.

An hour passes. He re-enters the kitchen.

"Smells good in here. You did a good job, Ba."

"Thanks. Listen, be careful what you put in that cabinet. You could forget it's down there."

"No, you're right, you're right. From now on, no more live food down there."

23 APRIL

He knocks on my door at 7:15 this morning.

"Ba, we're picking up Bill and Ralph ["Cynthia" for those new to the thread — keep up, will ya?] and going to the Cannery Casino Hotel at quarter to 11 for breakfast and lunch."

"What do you mean, 'and'?"

"We do both."

"Right. The slide."

"We get there at 10:45 or so, have breakfast, and then we hang around and slide right into lunch when they change over the buffet, which starts about 11:30. It's $4, but we get to eat two meals instead of one . . . four of us. You, me, Bill, and Ralph."

"We 'slide' into lunch?"

"Yeah. We've done it before."

CANNERY (Supplemental)

The whole operation has fallen apart. The buffet has staggered the end-breakfast/start-lunch times. Breakfast now ends at 10:30, the buffet is closed, they chase everyone out, and it doesn't reopen until 11:30. The end of "sliding."

My father is nonplussed.

"The miserable bastards!"

25 APRIL

My father's *Las Vegas Review-Journal* didn't come today. At first he thought it was because of some post-Easter holiday/newspaper-delivery-employee day off of which he was unaware.

"Hey, Ba, are they working today or what? Is it still Easter?"

He called the paper's customer service and was told it must have been a mistake.

"OK," I hear him say to the phone, "but if it doesn't come tomorrow, I'm calling back for a credit . . . for both days."

A few minutes later the phone rings.

"What do you mean, 'canceled'? Why? What? So call and tell me the credit card has expired. . . . You don't just stop the paper. Pick up the phone! . . . OK, you know what? Forget the whole thing. Cancel my subscription. I don't want any part of you."

And he hangs up. Well, he tries to, but the cordless in the living room isn't cooperating, so there are a number of attempts before the phone actually finds the cradle.

"Fuck 'em, fuck 'em. I need this?" he asks.

"Here's the problem, Dad. You kinda do. You like the cross-word puzzle every day. What are you going to do now?"

"I'll just go out and buy the paper."

"But that will cost you even more money and they'll still have your business."

"I just won't buy it every day."

Hours later, I return from meeting a friend for lunch.

"So while you were out, Ba, the woman at the paper says they want me back. I said, 'All right, what do you got for me?' She tells me $4.19 per month for three years."

"You broke them, Dad."

"You bet your ass. And I told them, 'You got a deal! But next time there's a problem, you call me first BEFORE you stop the paper, understand?' "

"And then what?"

"And she said whatever, whatever, but the point is, I went without a paper for one day, so I went out and bought one. No big deal. See, what happened was they canceled my paper, said my card wasn't good, but it was good, so I told them I'm finished, goodbye."

"Dad, I know. I was there, remember?"

"Were you here? Oh, yeah, that's right."

26 April

"You got a birthday today, don't you?"

"Wayne's is today. Mine is on May 3rd."

"Who the hell can remember? You're all so close together."

"Who told you and Mom to have sex that week in August?"

"Yeah, you're right."

Ever since they "moved the streets" at the airport (according to my father), it seemed wise for me to take a courtesy bus from the Suncoast Casino, five minutes from his house and, fortu-itously, where he bowls on Tuesdays and Fridays, to McCarran rather than let him drive me. He's inside now, practicing before league play. On the heels of the slide being impossible, the Suncoast Bowling Brain Trust is allowing each bowler only one soft drink — no refills!

"No more soda, Ba," my father informs me. "They only give you one lousy coupon now."

Miserable bastards.

Aside from the sadness that I always feel when I leave (the guilt, too, that I wasn't attentive enough or, yes, mocked him too much here), there is, as my sister once commented, the sickening sense I may not see him again. My rabbi mentioned once that when he was going in for triple-bypass surgery, he didn't feel it necessary to gather his family around to tell them how much he loved them.

"They know," he said, "they know."

That's the hope, right?

~

APRIL 28

Back in Tulsa

The phone rings.

"Happy birthday, Ba."

"Not today. Francesca, Wayne's daughter, your granddaughter, has a birthday today. Mine is on the 3rd."

"Well, happy early birthday to you."

"Thanks."

~

MAY 2014

~

1 MAY

The phone rings.

"So, you're 60 today!"

"Not today. It's Susan's birthday."

"Yours is today, your sister's is Saturday."

"No, Dad, Susan's is today, mine is Saturday."

"I know, I know, I got confused. I know one was on the first, one on the third, and between you and Wayne and Susan and Francesca having birthdays in the same week, who can keep track?"

"Right. And where did you get the idea I'm going to be 60?"

"No? I thought it was 50 or 60, I don't know."

(Gotta love a man who gives himself a 10-year cushion.)

"57."

"Jesus, you're getting old. And Wayne's 70."

"59. . . . You know, Dad, Susan's got a big one coming up."

"How old is she going to be?"

"50. Did you call her?"

"Yeah, yeah. She's 50, you know?"

"I think I just said that."

"Yeah, yeah, yeah. 50 . . . really?"

"Dad, did you really call?"

"I'm going to. I mean, I did."

"You did?"

"Well, not today."

"Well, today's her birthday, so it would be a good day."

"I did, I did."

"You just said you didn't."

"Well, I didn't yet. I can never reach her. Anyway, just thought I'd call, wish you a happy birthday."

"It's not my birthday, but you get credit for the call."

"Hey, listen, between you and Wayne and Susan and Francesca—"

"—I know. Who can keep track?"

2 MAY

~

THE PHONE RINGS. Yep.

"Just calling to wish you a happy birthday."

"Thanks, Dad, but still not my birthday. It's my ex-wife's birthday. Getting closer, though."

"Who? The singer?"

(My second wife is a singer-songwriter. Whenever my father mentions her, he mimes strumming an imaginary guitar by his chest.)

"Yes. Susan."

"I know, I know. Just calling to prepare you for tomorrow."

~

3 MAY

My birthday. He doesn't call.

6 MAY

He calls.

"Did you get the check?"

"No. You sent a check? You didn't have to do that. Thanks."

"I sent you a check for your birthday. I mailed it on Saturday. What the hell goes on with the mail?"

"It's Tuesday morning. Probably didn't go out until yesterday, which means it's too early to complain about the mail."

"Nah, New York, one day, the mail comes. Oklahoma, takes weeks sometimes."

"Hey, not for nothing, you called me every day last week and wished me a happy birthday except ON my birthday. A son could feel neglected."

"Oh, c'mon, I gotta call you on the actual day? You know, between Wayne and Susan—"

"—I know. I know."

"So, listen, I find when I drink more water, I feel better, meaning I don't feel quite so loogy."

"Loogy?"

"You know."

"Loogy?"

"Yeah, you know, loogy."

"I know what the word means, but I don't think it's what you want to say."

"And the pressure's down, and I'm feeling good . . . and I should have called you."

"No, it's all right, you got full credit for earlier calls."

"Yeah, I called you how many days? That's gotta count. Oh, Jeanine and I went to Primm."

Astonishing, isn't it?

"We've been there, Dad. We hated it."

"No, they had a buffet. Wow-we-wow! The variety! And I won $150 and I'm bowling today."

MAY 8

This time I call.

"Hey, Dad, got the check for the birthday. Very thoughtful."

"OK. You know, between you, Wayne, Susan — your birthdays are all in the same week. It's killing me."

"It's killing you?"

"You know what I mean. I'm going broke. You're on the 1st, Susan's the 3rd, Wayne's the 2nd."

It's easier just to agree sometimes.

"I know. It's a madhouse."

"And I didn't know what the hell to get you. Buy yourself something, OK?"

"I will. Thanks again."

"And don't get shook up. You all got the same amount."

10 MAY

In which the birthday saga continues.

To review: I got a birthday check; my brother, Wayne, got a birthday check; my niece, Francesca, Wayne's daughter, got a birthday check; my sister, Susan, no check.

I thought she took it well.

"It was my 50th birthday!" she says to me on the phone today. "That's it! I'm not getting him anything for Father's Day and I'm putting him in a home."

To ease the humiliation and pain, Wayne, who was in New York visiting, took her to dinner at Denny's.

16 MAY

The Birthday, Part Ad Infinitum

When my father discovered Susan had not received a birthday check, he sent a replacement. Before it arrived, however, Susan called and told him she had received the first check. It had been lost in the mail.

"Tell you what, Sue," he apparently told her, "just keep the second one too, when it arrives. Enjoy yourself."

I immediately called my father upon hearing the news.

"You sent Susan two checks and I get one? What kind of bullshit is this?"

"You know what? I'm done with all of you."

28 MAY

He calls.

"Ba, I'm putting on weight. I'm putting on weight. It's these goddamn buffets."

"But so what? You're 145 years old. Enjoy yourself. What are you worried about?"

"Enjoy myself? It's too much. Who can eat this much?"

"So stop going."

"Nah, I get the twofers. How do you not go? Lunch, dinner. They keep sending me coupons. What's making me fat?"

"The cakes and the cookies."

"I know, I know. I'm going to stay away from the cakes and cookies from now on. That's what's doing it."

"Good plan. Now, look, just to remind you. You said you'd move to Tulsa when you were 88 Well, this year you're 88."

"I'm changing it to 95."

"You can't change it. We had a deal."

"Talk to my attorney. As soon as he gets out of jail."

"You're killing me with that joke."

"All right, I'll come, I'll look around, but I'm telling you right now: I'm not moving into no dump."

MAY 31

After being told that Susan and her son, Chris; Wayne, Hope, and their daughter, Francesca; and Melissa, Gregory, and I will all be in Las Vegas to visit him, beginning on June 29th, he said, "Wow-we-wow, all of you here on the same day. Great! We'll go to dinner. Hey, who's picking up that check? Tell you what. I'll split it with you."

JUNE

6 JUNE

My mother, perhaps thinking about her own struggles with the everyday, used to say, "By your father, the sun shines." My father would respond, "Then, Flo, stand close."

He calls.

"Hey, Ba, I just won $838 at the South Point. It's a beautiful casino — well-lit, too. And they bought me a buffet dinner. Didn't even have to ask for a comp. They just gave me one."

"Dinner, too?"

"Yeah! I didn't really want it. I had a buffet yesterday, going to have one tomorrow, wasn't even that hungry, but what the hell, right?"

"Right."

There is a logic to free food, even when you're not hungry.

∾

14 JUNE (FATHER'S DAY)

He calls.

"Hello, Barry, I'm at the casino, I won $900, I'm bombed out of my mind, and they just gave me a buffet comp. I'm going to go eat now. Everything all right with you, sweetheart?"

"Hey, Dad, happy Father's Day."

"Oh, yeah, that's right. I'm the father."

∾

22 JUNE

I call.

"Morning, Dad, how are you?"

"I don't know, I haven't taken my pulse yet."

"You feeling all right?"

"Yeah, yeah, just woke up. Going to the buffet at the Suncoast later."

A little later, he calls.

"So what's the plan, again?"

"OK, so next Sunday, we'll all be there. Wayne and Hope said they want to cook a meal."

"Your brother with these health foods," he says. "They are the most — what can I say? — most un-delectable foods I have ever tasted in my life. It's not that the food's bad, don't misunderstand me, but what's the word I'm looking for? You're a writer."

"Taste?"

"Yes, that's it. He buys me oatmeal. It's dry, I can't eat it. OK, I mean, I don't eat that much oatmeal anyway."

Later in the day, I call.

"I have to tell you, Dad, people on Facebook love you."

"What, what, what are you writing? You mean our escapades are that interesting to people?"

"Well, you are."

"Did you know these people before me?"

"Yes. They're my friends."

"Oh, I thought maybe you met them after me."

❀

23 JUNE

He calls.

"So, you still coming?" he asks.

"Yes, still coming."

"Still coming Sunday?"

"Still coming Sunday."

"Time. I need a time. You have a flight number? I don't know when you're coming. Give me a time, for crying out loud!"

"Afternoon, around one, but don't worry, Susan's picking us up. I told you, remember?"

"C'mon! I can come to the airport. She doesn't have to come."

"She'll be at the airport, anyway, flying in."

"You know she's flying in Sunday?"

"Yeah, that's why, uh——"

"You don't want me to come?"

"You don't have to come. Besides, it's a madhouse down there. They moved the roads, remember?"

"I won't park. I'll just pull up to the place where you pull up. You know where it is — that place near the whatchamacallit. We'll meet there."

"Really, Susan's renting a car. We'll be there at the same time. You don't need to come."

"She knows when you're coming?"

"Yeah."

"You told her?"

"Yeah, I told her."

"All right, I'll be here. I'll stick around the house. Ba, it's so stinking hot. Wow-we-wow! The sun, it's murder. You can't go outside. You sure you don't want me to come?"

"I don't."

"Why?"

"Susan is going to be there."

"You sure?"

"Yes."

"She told you that?"

"Yes."

∿

24 JUNE

"Hey, Dad, where were you today?"

"Bowling."

"Bowling? You don't bowl on Thursdays."

"Yeah, I know. Just went down to practice."

"Practice? You keep this up, you'll dominate the 90-plus league someday."

"What do you want me to tell you? Wait — they have such a league?"

28 June

We're all arriving in Las Vegas today: Susan, her kids; Wayne, Hope, Francesca; Melissa, Gregory, and I. I called in the morning to plan, what else, dinner that night. My father had previously expressed some concern over this.

"Don't worry, Dad, we'll bring Chinese in tonight."

"Yes, yes, yes, yes, yes! You mean . . . oh, yeah! Great idea. Which Chinese place?"

"The one near you."

"Yes! Oh, they make an egg foo young. It's enormous. Too much for one person. We'll share it."

That night. We arrive.

"Melissa," my father asks, "how goes your life?"

"Good, Jack. Yours?"

"You used to be a blonde."

"Not for a while."

"You looked better. Go back."

Dinner, and yes, he's right, the egg foo young is enormous. My father then announces his favorite Father's Day present. Wayne bought him coffee from Starbucks, I got him a gift certificate from Best Buy, but the winner . . .

"Susan, this plastic shoe horn is great. You don't have to bend down. It's fabulous. It's so long. The others you have to do like this [he begins to bend] but not with this one. You can sit like this [he sits straight]. Thank you so much!"

30 June

There's a Spanish music channel on DirectTV and my father is wearing a wavy blond toupee. That is all for today.

JULY 2014

∾

1 JULY

For reasons that defy understanding, Wayne, my father, and I are watching European soccer.

"What's the matter? You can't use your hands?" my father screams. Then, seeing the Belgium coach, he yells, "Get off the field, you hockey puck!" and in the next breath he turns to Melissa, who walks into the room and is wearing a gray tank top, and says, "Get the next size. You're busting out all over."

3 JULY

Before heading to the Bagel Cafe, my father is in the living room listening to Rock en español.

"You know," he says in the car, "Savas is a Greek. What's he doing in a Jewish place?"

"How many times are you going to tell us this?" I ask.

"I just thought you'd like to know. What a grouch! I won't tell you anymore."

"Yes, you will."

After breakfast, we all decide to head to Hoover Dam. If you bet the "Under" (+/- 7.5) on the number of times my father was going to say, "Damn Dam," I'm sorry for your loss.

(Pro tip: Never bet the "Under" when it comes to my father.)

Later he wins $156 at the Suncoast.

"I shouldn't drink so much, Ba, I just shouldn't," he says on the way home. The rest of the family decided not to join us. "Well, when I say, 'a lot,' I mean I didn't drink THAT much."

"How many did you have tonight?"

"Well, I was playing blackjack, I was up, down, up, down. I had four gin-and-tonics, but that's not my point."

"That's not your point? That should be your point."

"I always feel lousy afterwards. I shouldn't drink. But I sleep better."

"You all right? You seem preoccupied this week."

"Preoccupied? No, I'm just thinking a lot."

"That's pretty much the definition of preoccupation, Dad."

"Nah, not preoccupied. I'm a planner. I plan."

"What are you planning?"

"Nothing. But I'm a planner."

"OK, you're a planner."

"You know a lot of people my age think about the big blah."

"The big blah?"

"That doom and gloom is around the corner."

"You think about the big blah?"

"What are you talking about?"

"The big blah. You said something about the big blah."

"No, I'm just thinking. Where do you want to go for breakfast tomorrow?"

4 JULY

In which Jack Friedman doesn't want to move the Styrofoam head.

Perhaps an explanation is in order. My mother was a costume designer and, as such, had mannequins and Styrofoam heads about the house. One such head made it to Las Vegas when my father moved, which he put outside the living room window, so that those driving by can see.

Don't ask.

Anyway, on the Styrofoam head, he put a straw cowboy hat and sunglasses, which is where we begin because my father has finally agreed to start getting the house in shape to sell it, meaning the head may lose its place at chez Friedman.

"I don't want to move anything around the house. And why do I have to move it?"

"Because, Dad, Bruce Simons, my friend, your real estate agent, thinks, and I agree, it's a little disconcerting to potential buyers to see this head out there."

"I don't follow you. What's the problem with it?"

"Dad, you have a Styrofoam mannequin head in one of the windows, looking out, and it's wearing a straw cowboy hat and sunglasses."

"I like it! It's unique. Who has that kind of thing?"

His logic, once again, is unassailable.

At dinner tonight, he once again brings up the national spoon shortage.

5 JULY

Upon finishing his generic frosted flakes from the Dollar Store and his coffee with Half & Half and four Sweet 'n Lows, I tell him I'm going to get bagels. "Bagels?" he says. "They're too heavy in the morning. You can't eat like that. All right, we'll go. But I can't eat a whole bagel. Maybe just a poppy."

Later that day:

My son died in 2008 at 24. My father knew Paul, but they didn't see each other much. I don't pretend to know how a grandfather deals with the death of his grandson, generally, and how much Jack Friedman, this grandfather, has dealt with the death of his grandson, specifically. He doesn't mention Paul much, hardly ever, actually, except a few times when he wants me to review how many children I have. My daughter, Nina, is remembered by my father most of the time. At times, my father's inability or unwillingness to deal with my son's death, or even mention it, seems cruel, but it's not, even though it can be hard to remember that. Once, he asked, "Hey, Ba, how many kids you have?" "Two," I answered, "but Paul died." "Well, he doesn't count. No, I mean how many do you have living?"

This afternoon, though, my dad was asleep on the sofa. He woke up suddenly. He looked confused, hurt.

"Dad, what is it?"

"Where's Paul, Barry?" he asked about his first grandchild. "Where's Paul?"

6 July

He is up early, before 7:00, watching tennis, screaming at the crowds at Wimbledon for never applauding about HIS backhand and at Novak Djokovic for not having a more pronounceable name ("What kind of fakakta name is that?"). He tells me Bill will pick him up for lunch at 10:30 a.m.

"Why so early?" I ask.

"I gotta get you to the airport."

"Our flight's at 6:25 tonight. You'll be fine."

"I'm worried about traffic," he says.

"You'll be back by 12:30 or 1:00. Don't worry."

He gets back at 12:15. We leave for the airport at 2:30.

"The problem with all these signs," he says on the way, "you have to read them. There's just too goddamn many of them."

"Don't read them."

"I don't, I don't. I'm just saying they're here."

Costco . . . Pep Boys . . . Honda . . . Whole Food . . . Orleans Casino.

"Orleans? Like New Orleans? What's it doing in Vegas? Did you settle up at the front desk before you left the house?" he asks Melissa.

"Yes, I did," she responds, playing along.

"Did you use water?"

"Wasn't that included in the reservation?"

"I have to charge you extra for that."

～

12 JULY

He calls around 4 p.m.

"It's so goddamn hot here. You can't go out. It's murder."

"What are you going to do, then?"

"Ah, I'm going out."

"Where?"

"Dinner with Jeannette."

"You got it right."

"What?"

"Nothing."

"When are you going?"

"Four."

"So early?"

"She eats early, what can I tell you?"

"Buffet?"

"Yeah, but I gotta stop. They're killing me. I'm putting on so much weight on account of these buffets, I'm afraid I'm not going to fit in the coffin."

"Dad, we're going to cremate you."

"All right, very good. Just make sure I'm dead so I don't feel the fire. But this is a good buffet, so what the hell? How's the weather there?"

"It's hot."

"Well, baby, it's summer. What are you going to do?"

22 JULY

He calls.

The conversation turns to my new electric car, a Nissan Leaf.

"So you're telling me you just plug the car in?"

"Yeah."

"How do I know when it needs juice?"

"It'll tell you."

"What, I'm going to have to look? I want to run, I run. I don't want to have to do that."

"You look at a gas gauge now, right?"

"Yeah, but that's different. What if I want to drive to New York?"

"You would never drive to New York. It's 3,000 miles."

"But say I did. Could I do it? Would I just charge it up at the hotel every night along the way?"

"The range isn't there yet. My car only gets about 75 miles per full charge."

"But if I wanted to."

"Yeah, if you could find charging stations. But even then, it would take you a few months to get there, as it takes about four hours to charge each time."

"That's not the point — I'd probably fly."

~

23 JULY

My father called to tell me he's coming to Tulsa for a visit around Rosh Hashanah.

"Hey, Ba," he said when he called back with the reservation info, "you got Jews there?"

~

28 JULY

He calls.

"Ba, I'm having a good couple of wins at the casinos. $100 here, $100 there. Nothing special, but listen to this: The Boyd Properties are offering a $7.77 buffet, and that's for breakfast, lunch AND dinner . . . at every hotel. And I got twofers! You know what I'm talking about here? Two people get to eat for that price. I'm having steak, chicken cacciatore every meal. It's too much, I'm gaining weight, but at that price, how do you not go and eat three meals a day there?"

"You can't, Dad. You simply can't."

AUGUST 2014

∼

9 AUGUST

I call.

"Hey, Dad, what's going on?"

"It is murderous out here, Ba, this heat. But everything is cool. I feel good, no lie, but you can't go out. What are you going to do? Who put this city in a desert, anyway? No other place to put it, but bowling is good. I had a 514 series. Two more weeks in the summer league, then we start the fall league. I enjoy it. And I'm buffeting it—"

"Buffeting?"

"You know what I mean, but I'm putting on weight. My pants are getting tight . . . and tomorrow, what's-her-name and I and Bill and, uh—"

"Cynthia."

"Cynthia are going to Primm. It's 10 bucks for the bus, but they buy you a buffet lunch, so what the hell?"

"You go there a lot."

"I know, I know. Just thought I'd tell you. Bill, he loves the buffets, wow-we-wow, can he eat! Looking forward to seeing you in September because, you know, that's when I fly. I'll take the bus from the Suncoast. Listen, if you come out for that thing you told me about, make sure you tell me. All I do is gamble and eat, eat and gamble. Today, I won $14. But everything is cool. I have the Coumadin Clinic end of the month, I have to give blood. The levels are good. And you and Melissa, OK? Gregory and the ex-husband? One question on the cellphone: Where are my phone numbers? You know the list, I can't find 'em. It's no big deal, I don't need them, but maybe you'll show me in September. I want to make a goddamn call, I can't find the number. Do I have to dial '1' on the phone? No, that's right, I don't. On the home phone I do. And, look, if I'm not home, leave the message, because I'm running all over the place. But everything is cool. And you, you working or what? You making money?"

One breath! Damn!

~

12 AUGUST

He calls.

"This goddamn Century Link sends me a bill for twice what it should be, so I called to let them know to fix their goddamn billing department."

"What did they say?"

"Nothing. Couldn't get them on the phone. Talked to a recording. It told me to call during normal business hours, so I hung up."

"When did you call?"

"Just now."

"It's 6:30 in the morning."

"Yeah, maybe you're right. I'll call later."

14 AUGUST

He calls.

"Hey, Ba, I'm at the Red Rock, because every Monday in August, veterans get two-for-one at the buffet. You've been there, right?"

"Yes."

"Yeah, that's right. When were you here?"

"With you."

"Yeah, yeah."

"But why Mondays? Why in August?"

"Who the hell knows? So what's new with you, sweetheart?"

"Things are OK. Little stressed, I—"

"—What are you going to do, baby? That's life. We don't know from nothing. Someone makes the plans and God doesn't say a word. Anyway, everything's cool, feeling good, say hello to Melissa and Gregory, and stay in touch."

25 AUGUST

He calls.

"Listen, I know you called the last couple of days, but I got so busy with this, with that, I didn't call you back. And it's so goddamn hot here. Wow-we-wow! Anyway, everything's cool. So, yeah, I know you called. I sit down to call you back, but then something comes up, business or pleasure — hee-hee — and I forget to call. Anyway, I get stuff from clients, you know, accounting work, blah-blah-blah. I can't read their writing, their records are from hunger, so I say 'the hell with it,' and I run. But everything is cool, the levels are good, feeling good, but my legs. I can't play tennis! The legs. They don't work. Anyway, so don't worry if you call and I'm not here, I'm probably out. But, really, Ba, everything's cool. How about you?"

"Well, you know—"

"—All right, talk to you soon. Thank you for the call."

27 AUGUST

He calls.

"Barry, this goddamn computer! I just want to get some tax forms."

"Did you go online?"

"What do you mean . . . where?"

"The computer, you know, the internet. What are you trying to find?"

"Where?" he asks.

"What do you mean, 'where?' "

"Where?" he asks again.

"Where what, Dad?"

"Where do you mean? What am I looking for?"

"The computer — on the desk."

"Yeah, I have it on the desk. What's your point? You know, I have two desks."

"I'm aware. Click the Google icon and then you'll get to Gmail."

"The who?"

"I'm going to send you an email."

"How do I get that?"

"You know how to get your email."

"It says 'FAX.' "

"Are you looking at the computer?"

"What? Yeah. . . . No, I'm looking at the fax machine."

"The computer is on the other desk."

"I know. I have two. All right, I'm there. Now, where's the icon? Where are my icons? And what's Google? What kind of name is Google?"

"Don't worry about the name now."

"I know, I know. I'm just wondering. OK, I got something. What am I looking at?"

"I don't know. I'm not there. What do you see?

"I see 'From Barry, To Jack, Visit my website: www.barrysfriedman.com.' What's that?"

"My website."

"Your what?"

"Don't worry about that now."

"I'm not worried about it — I want Form 1120. Why are they making this so difficult? What's this? What kind of fakakta stupid letter is this? 'Typhoon relief efforts in the Philippines.' What the hell is this?"

"Must be a deduction you can take."

"What happened in the Philippines? They had a typhoon? You know I was in the Philippines in the war."

"You're killing me."

We hang up.

An hour and 10 minutes later, the phone rings.

"Ba, I got everything. I'm not going to even do the stupid taxes now. I'm going to go get something to eat. Look, I'm sorry it's so frustrating. But something was going on. I'm not blaming you. Probably it's me."

∾

September 2014

∾

2 September

He calls.

"Hey, Ba, when my fax machine is off, will I still get my emails?"

"You mean your faxes."

"No, the Epsom. I can't get an email, uh, fax. OK, which is which?"

"Just leave everything on."

"But there's a light on the Epsom. Does that mean it's on?"

"Yes."

"So, I'll get my emails?"

"Yeah."

"Oh, listen to this, the Red Rock now has twofers for veterans every Monday, and that's for all the properties. Every Monday for a solid month, and then when the month ends, I can get another card for a solid month. When you come, we'll go.

You've been there, right? $7.77, we both eat. How do you beat that?"

"Are there any casinos not offering the $7.77 special?"

"What do you mean?"

"The other casino is too. You told me."

"I told you?"

"You told me."

"When did I tell you?"

"When? I don't know when. But you did."

"I don't remember. Anyway, this stupid cellphone, I can't make a call in the casino. I don't have the number anyway, but, still, to make a goddamn call. And nobody can hear me, they say I don't pick up. I think the ringer's off."

"It's the reception inside, it's not you. We'll turn the ringer on, or make it louder, when you get here."

"I can do it. Just tell me what to do. I mean, I don't use the cell outside of the house anyway. And I had a good week, I won 40, 50, 40 and then the big one . . . 1,100."

"Great."

"I did a couple of big tax returns and nothing. But I can't get these guys to pay me. I mean, they send what they send, but . . . uh, listen, I'll get it. They're good for it. They always pay. But this goddamn phone. And Century Link keeps sending me bills. Who's Century Link?"

"Your internet company."

"All right, I don't use it much. I come to you on the 23rd, you know."

"Looking forward to it."

"OK, but I was just worried, so when I come to you, leave the Epsom on, correct, and I'll get my emails?"

"Absolutely."

~

13 September

A few days back, my father experienced some numbness in his feet and hands, so Bill drove him to the hospital, where he was diagnosed with spinal stenosis, a narrowing of the open spaces of the spine, which can manifest symptoms such as numbing. It can be instigated by things as simple as putting on one's shoes.

"Ba," my father said when he returned home, "I'm going to get some slip-ons, no more with the laces, and I'm just not going to look down anymore. No more bending — that's all."

23 September

He arrives. He's hungry.

On the way to Village Inn from the airport, he says, "You remember Sol, he married Muriel — she's a Jewish girl, by the way — anyway, he's very impressed by you. I don't know why."

24 September

On the way to B'nai Emunah, here in Tulsa, for Rosh Hashanah services:

"Dad, I'm glad you're here."

"All right. Hey, how many times a day do you get in and out of this car?"

"I don't know. Three times. Why?"

"Get a job already! Jesus!"

"L'shanah tovah!"

"What?"

"I was wishing you a happy — ah, forget it."

"In what, Jewish?"

"Hebrew."

25 September

Still in Tulsa.

We are sitting at an intersection. To our right is a place called Harvard Meats, which is all you need to know about today's installment.

"Hey, Ba, what kind of name is Harvard Meats?"

"What kind?"

"Who names a place Harvard Meats?"

"People who own a meat store on Harvard, I guess."

"We're on Harvard?"

"Yeah."

"Is it good meat?"

"Pretty good."

"So you've been there?"

"Yeah, that's how I know."

"Harvard . . . Harvard! Is that permitted? Does Harvard know?"

"Does Harvard . . . I don't know."

"What kind of meat do they have? The usual? I mean, the meats and the chicken."

"I guess."

"How is it better from other meats?"

"I don't know that it is."

"Harvard Meats, nu? You give yourself a name?"

28 September

Before my father came to Tulsa this time, but after it was decided he would move here permanently, I planned a party for him at the house. Friends, and friends of friends, and people who follow these stories on Facebook were all invited. I made the mistake of telling him about it.

"Am I going to have to give a speech?"

"Not if you don't want to."

"Are people bringing presents or cash?"

"I don't think they're bringing either."

"Why not?"

We went to dinner tonight and my father, doing his act, as he does, was stymied by someone else's word choice.

"Would you like coffee, sir?" the waitress asked.

"Do I? Is the pope Catholic?"

"No, sir, he's not," she responded, "he's Argenteeny."

29 September

Leaving Tulsa.

Two women approach my father and me at the bagel place.

"Are you . . . Barry?" one asks me.

I nod.

"I know you, I know you," the other one says to my father, tapping him on the shoulder. "You were in the paper. Hey, Carol, look who it is. I know Jack! We know Jack!"

"I'm the father."

"We know."

"This is my son."

"We know."

"You know I'm the father?" he asks.

∼

OCTOBER 2014

∼

15 OCTOBER

The house on Tumble Brook Drive sells. He'll make about 30 grand when it's all settled. The first buyer backed out when he discovered my father didn't have both the heating and air-conditioning unit replaced — just the heater.

"What the hell happened again?" my father asked when I told him the deal fell through.

"You told the guy you had both the AC and heater replaced, and he thought he was getting new."

"That's why he canceled?"

"Yeah. Kind of a big deal."

"C'mon, I didn't have to replace the heater."

"It wasn't working, you kind of did."

"Ach! And these new people?"

"We told them the heater wasn't new."

"Who told them?"

"Vicki, your real-estate agent, my friend."

"Lou's Vicki? Vicki Mustard."

"No, my Vicki."

"You have a Vicki?"

"Sort of. She's your Vicki too."

28 OCTOBER

He calls.

"Hey, Ba, listen, about the house and this move. So the movers are going to come whenever they come, and then the next day we move, right? By the way, this is Dad."

November 2014

~

1 November

"Ba, I'm going through stuff. I have the office supplies I have to pack."

"What do you mean?"

"You know, the envelopes, the copy paper."

"We have those in Oklahoma, you know. You don't have to move that stuff."

"No, I mean the big ones — the Manila envelopes."

"We have those, too. Pens, labels, really. Got it all."

"You sure?"

"Trust me."

"In Oklahoma? You're not civilized there. Oklahoma isn't a state, it's a condition."

5 November

After hearing him on the phone the past few days and how overwhelmed he sounded, I decided to head to Las Vegas to help him pack.

"I want to do something light for dinner," he says on the first night. "Nothing heavy. I can't eat these big meals anymore. I'm done with the buffets."

"You're not done with the buffets."

"Well, when I say 'done,' I don't mean I'm not going."

"Thanks for clearing that up. You want a salad?"

"Nah."

"Soup?"

"I fill up on soup."

"But not if you're not eating anything else."

"Yeah, you're right. But soup? I don't know. Yes, no . . . I don't know."

"A burger?"

"No! Light, light! I can't eat these big meals. Who can eat this much? I don't have the appetite I used to when I was playing tennis every day."

"What sounds good, then?"

"I don't know. How about the shrimp egg foo young from that place? It's the best I've ever had. And with the sauce they give you, I'm telling you. You ever had it?"

"Isn't it heavy, though? They give you three patties."

"I'm not going to have the three patties. It's too much. I'll have what's left for lunch tomorrow."

6 November

Vicki Arnold Simons and Bruce Simons, his real-estate agents extraordinaire, just stopped by.

"You know," he says to Vicki, "there's you, Vicki Schwartz, and Vicki Mustard. I know three. Vicki Schwartz was a girl I was running with, Vicki Mustard married Lou Ferruci, and now there's you."

"Yes," she says, "you've told me before."

"Is your name 'Vicki' short for Vivian?"

"Actually, my name is Victoria."

"Oh," he says. "My sister's name was Vivian, but she died."

Later we head to the Suncoast with Bill. They are discussing their Veterans Day plans . . . five days away.

"We're going to have to get there early," Bill says.

"The buffet will be mobbed."

"I'll pick you up at two, OK? Just want to double-check. We're going to the Red Rock, right?"

"It's the best one," says my father.

"Just curious, what time do they start serving dinner?"

"4:30," says Bill.

"Make sure you two get plenty of rest," I say.

7 November

"Jennifer made these goddamn cookies," he says to me this afternoon, "and I ate two or three. I knew when I was eating them, I shouldn't. I said to myself, 'Don't eat the cookies! They're going to sit right here [taps his chest].' And sure enough, bingo, I get this. Who told her to make cookies? Nu? Cookies, she makes. And they were the ones with the thick dough. Not good. Not good at all."

"Maybe she's trying to kill you," I say, trying to lighten his mood.

"Nah, it's not that."

He answers me.

Just then he points to a three-foot-tall plastic Coca-Cola bottle filled with pennies in his office.

"Hey, Ba, where can I cash in these pennies?"

"Vons."

"Vons?"

"Vons."

"What do you mean, 'Vons'?"

"Vons, the grocery store."

"What about them?"

"It's where you can cash in your pennies. They have a counter."

"A counter?"

"A machine."

"What?"

"A machine that counts."

"Where?"

"Vons."

"I know."

"No, you don't."

"Well, I thought they did. I mean, I've seen those machines. But they take eight percent. Why should I give them eight percent?"

"Don't you think it's worth it?"

"You know what? Forget it. We'll just put the pennies in the trunk of the car when we move to Tulsa. I'll cash them in when I get there."

"You want to drive the pennies to Tulsa?"

10 November

My father is standing firm. The pennies are not moving, and what started out as slight banter and where one might want to cash in thousands of pennies from a plastic Coke bottle is now a full-fledged kerfuffle.

"We're not cashing them in, Ba," he says, after seeing how much it will cost at Vons. Yes, we took the pennies to Von's to check to see if it's worth cashing them in — not to actually cash them in.

"You're really going to schlep the Coke bottle to Tulsa?" I ask on the way back to the house.

"Yeah, we'll leave them in the car."

"Are you nuts?"

"What are you getting shook up about? They're MY pennies."

11 November

"Hey, listen, baby," he says to me on the way to one of the veterans buffets, "don't make fun of that bridge that fell on my toe. That was a famous bridge. That was the bridge in *The Bridge on the River Kwai*."

"It was not that bridge. Jesus!"

"Well, no, not exactly that bridge. The Kwai Bridge wasn't in the Philippines. It was in Thailand. I was in the Philippines."

"Close enough, though, right?"

"But it was a good movie. Made a star of what's-his-name. Who was in that picture?"

"William Holden?"

"Yeah, yeah. He died."

13 November

Denny's in Summerlin. Late night.

"Oh, bless you, my dear," he says as the waitress brings him his decaf, "may you never know the horrors of stretch marks."

"More Half & Half?" she asks.

"Is Bismarck a herring? Is 58 the atomic weight of cobalt?"

It never gets old.

14 November

At Golden Dragon on Tropicana in Las Vegas, it's all you can eat for $11.50 but ... it's not a buffet. You order off the menu and eat as much as you want. That's the good news! The bad news is you have to finish what you order or a) you don't get to order anything else, and b) if you don't finish, the $11.50 is null and void and all that you've ordered reverts back to a la carte pricing. Think about the ramifications of 12 pot stickers, egg drop soup, egg rolls, and chicken and cashews for $11.50, if managed successfully, and $37.50 if it's not. It's a lot of pressure.

My father's fortune, by the way, read, "You are very concerned with public service."

His response: "No, I'm not. I want a new fortune."

This, too, over egg rolls:

"Ba, thank you again for all that you did these last two weeks about the move and whatnot. I know you've got all the time in the world, but still, you did a lot."

∿

21 November

I'm back in Tulsa.

He calls.

"Hey, Ba, I need a city map of Tulsa."

"A city map?"

"Yeah, a map of Tulsa. You know, streets. You got something like that?"

"Yeah."

"So, you can get me one? I think they're called 'city maps.' That way I'll know where the hell I'm going. I mean, where do you get one of those?"

"City maps?"

"Yeah, of the streets. You know, you've seen them. It gives you the streets. It's a map."

"Dad, I got it, really. I'll look for you."

"Like in a five-and-dime store."

"A five and dime . . . yeah, that's where I'll look. You know they have maps online, too, these city maps."

"Yeah, yeah, I used it in Vegas. I get it on the computer. You got one in Tulsa, too?"

"We do."

"But, anyway, I want a map. You know what I'm talking about?"

"Yeah, I do, really I do. But all these maps are online, just so you know."

"Yeah, yeah, I know, but I'd like one I can have. You know—"

"—I know!"

"Some kind of map that'll show me around, that's all."

. . .

December 2014

~

2 December

Maybe it's the move to Tulsa, the sense that this, as I once heard it, will be the last stop on the train for my father.

"You get me back to your mother, I don't care what," he has said many times this month about wanting to be buried next to his wife, my mother, in a Long Island cemetery. "I don't care what it costs."

"I know, I know," I told him. "Don't worry."

"And if I run out of money, tell you what, burn me."

"Burn you?"

"Burn me!"

"Oh, you want to be cremated?"

"Yeah."

"We can do that. Have you cremated, put you in an urn, and then when I go up to New York, whenever that is, take the urn and, what, sprinkle your ashes over Mom's grave?"

"Just make sure I'm dead first."

~

22 December

He calls.

"Barry, speak up, I can't hear you."

"I haven't said anything yet."

"What?"

"I didn't say anything."

"I can't hear you."

"Dad?"

He hangs up.

~

25 December

He calls.

"How are you, Dad?"

"Merry Christmas, Ba."

"We're Jewish."

"What?"

"We're Jewish."

"All right, so festive Purim to you. You know, we gave them a God."

"Here we go."

"Yes, Mary and Joe Schwartz couldn't find a room at the inn and so they went to the uh, you know. And I gotta tell you, she's a virgin and gives birth? Doesn't work, baby."

"Go on."

"Jesus was born Jewish. It wasn't until later that he converted and gave them a religion. When I tell my friends that, Bill, Carole, Jeannette, they get all shook up."

"Imagine that."

"Oh and I filed my taxes early."

"How did you do that?"

"I electrified them."

"Nice."

"Did you get a notice that the returns were accepted?"

"Yes."

"Well done."

"You're telling me the IRS had a guy there this late, checking returns, and he did it that fast?"

~

29 December

Chris, Susan's second-oldest boy, early twenties, calls. My father is in New York, visiting Susan and her family.

"We're watching Jerry Springer, and it's a show about three

lesbians and some tension among the three, one in particular," Chris says.

"And?" I ask.

"Grandpa decided it was the fault of one of the lesbians because he kept pointing and saying, 'Kill her,' 'Kill her,' every time she appeared on the screen."

We found out, on the day the sale of his house was supposed to close, that the buyers backed out. Vicki found a new buyer almost immediately, but the closing was put off until the end of January 2015, which is where I will pick up this story in the next book.

Oh, in case you're wondering, he had $93 in pennies. Von's took eight percent, or $7.44. I then had to break the news to him.

"Dad, I cashed in the pennies."

"How much, how much?"

"About $93. Von's took almost eight."

"Miserable bastards."

ACKNOWLEDGMENTS

To all of you. You all have (had) fathers, yet you jumped into my world as if it were your own. The energy and love and interest you gave my father and his family was beautiful and touching and surprising. Without my father, obviously, there's no book. Without your particular joy in all things Jack Friedman, there isn't one either. To Bill for pushing everything else off his table to get this book done and to Tom Walsh for being so good at what he does.

And to Melissa.

ABOUT THE AUTHOR

An essayist, reporter, and political columnist, Barry Friedman's work has appeared in Esquire, where he has co-hosted "The Politics Blog with Charles P. Pierce" (Pierce in fact gave him the name "Friedman of the Plains"); The Progressive Populist; Inside Media; The Las Vegas Review-Journal; and AAPG EXPLORER, a magazine for petroleum geologists, which is all the more noteworthy, considering he knows little about petroleum geology and has hurt himself pumping his own gas. Further, Barry has appeared in national commercials, a few local ones, including a local pizza joint, which featured him lying on his back, facing and barking at a pizza. He does radio commentary on Public Radio and appeared in *UHF* with "Weird Al" Yankovic, setting the bar for all those who might someday play a character named "Thug #2." The movie still provides him with $3.76 residual checks every time it plays at some Lithuanian drive-in.

You can find out more about Barry at barrysfriedman.com and barrysfriedman.substack.com.

ALSO BY BARRY FRIEDMAN